SERIES EDITOR
Meenakshi Thapan

A series on EDUCATION AND SOCIETY IN SOUTH ASIA is, perhaps, somewhat ambitious given the magnitude and scope of the theme in present times. Instead of seeking to provide a narrow focus, it is hoped that a broad framework will allow the inclusion of work that seeks to understand education and society in both institutional and non-institutional frameworks. Institutional frameworks bring in a focus on schools and institutions for higher education as spaces within which educational processes and activities unfold. Non-institutional spaces include all those other social, cultural, and political spaces where pedagogic encounters of different kinds take place. They also include movements, trajectories, and patterns of different kinds that enable children and youth to learn and grow in unconventional ways. One of the lens through which this series aims to develop the sociology of education is through a focus on children and youth and aspects of their experience both within and outside institutional spaces.

At one level, this series seeks to problematize our understanding of education, *as process*, in the context of the making of citizens in a 'modern', changing South Asia. Most efforts view schools, for example, as institutions that transmit and evaluate educational knowledge and provide certification based on academic achievement. The causes of inequality, located in gender, caste, class, and religion have been examined in this context as these shape individuals' lives in multiple and complex ways. At the same time, schools and institutions for tertiary education are spaces, as *processes*, through which participants bring meaning and create worlds that hugely impact their personal and intellectual development.

Educational spaces are also about place and location in multiple ways, whether these are at the intersection of caste, gender, and class or are about location as both territorial and imagined spaces in the region. The sociology of education must unpack these complexities and bring out their implications in a variety of contexts in both rural and urban South Asia. The significance of gender, caste, religion, or language as defining characteristics of educational processes are germane to our understanding and need to be examined in different contexts in the region that make each experience unique and similar at the same time.

Conflict, crises, and events in everyday life are significant aspects of these processes. The ways in which youth may be both shaped by as well as engage with the unfolding of crises, events, and everyday life remain opaque in our understanding of how education plays an important role in the making of citizens in contemporary South Asia. It is this understanding of human agency in institutional contexts that has somehow eluded those arguments that over-emphasize the significance of the structural and ideological frameworks within which educational processes are embedded. Once we understand that students are keen and active participants in the processes in which they are inserted, our views about education and its possible outcomes may perhaps change. It is indeed possible to examine and understand the vastly differing and multiple practices that students engage in as agents within and outside an institutional framework. We need to, for example, focus on and unravel the complexities prevalent in understanding youth as active citizens in an increasingly cosmopolitan and interconnected world. How do they seek to rise above not just the normative expectations associated with their 'roles' as students but also with asserting themselves in deeply meaningful and contextually significant ways? This means that we must pay attention to critical consciousness as it reveals itself in pedagogic encounters of different kinds but also in peer cultures and student led organizations and movements in different parts of South Asia.

The goal is to sharpen our understanding of perspectives that do not rely on educational misgivings, institutional features, financial outlays, and state failures alone. These are only some social aspects of educational practice. There are other dimensions that envelop students, teachers, the community, and society in complex ways that we need to uncover in order to provide an understanding of how education and society connect in diverse ways.

Teachers are agents of both change as well as reproduction in education. It is important to identify and examine some of the processes that enable them to be pioneers and facilitators for transformative practices rather than only being viewed as toothless agents of the state or private bodies, as they usually are, without any possibilities for bringing about change. Both teachers and students are engaged participants in processes pertaining to education and the series needs to unpack the possibilities and potential for *movement* underlying the constrained and encapsulated worlds they inhabit. In this context, a focus on mainstream educational processes that incorporate a social, ecological, and moral vision for inclusive education is an endeavour for the series to document practices that focus on the well-being and holistic growth of all stakeholders in a changing and globalizing society.

EDUCATION AND SOCIETY IN SOUTH ASIA

SERIES EDITOR
Meenakshi Thapan

In Search of a Future

Andrea Kölbel

In Search of a Future

Youth, Aspiration, and Mobility in Nepal

Andrea Kölbel

OXFORD
UNIVERSITY PRESS

OXFORD
UNIVERSITY PRESS

Oxford University Press is a department of the University of Oxford.
It furthers the University's objective of excellence in research, scholarship,
and education by publishing worldwide. Oxford is a registered trademark of
Oxford University Press in the UK and in certain other countries.

Published in India by
Oxford University Press
22 Workspace, 2nd Floor, 1/22 Asaf Ali Road, New Delhi 110 002, India

© Oxford University Press 2020

The moral rights of the author have been asserted.

First Edition published in 2020

ISBN-13 (print edition): 978-0-19-012451-9
ISBN-10 (print edition): 0-19-012451-2

ISBN-13 (eBook): 978-0-19-099097-8
ISBN-10 (eBook): 0-19-099097-X

Typeset in Adobe Garamond Pro 11/13
by Tranistics Data Technologies, New Delhi 110 044
Printed in India by Rakmo Press, New Delhi 110 020

Contents

Figures

Preface

As this book goes to press, the young Nepalis who are at the centre of this study have found their futures. The conversations we had in Kathmandu in 2011–12 took place at a time when these young people faced a number of decisions which, they felt, would set the course for their future lives. The decisions are made. They are no longer the subject of debate. Yet, the arguments and the findings presented in this book continue to be of topical interest because they elucidate one of the conundrums at the core of social scientific debates about young people's role in processes of social change. Young people are commonly found to be highly aspirational as regards their potential futures and, at the same time, they are acutely aware of a range of persisting constraints that make it unlikely for them to realize their hopes for a better future. Educational expansion, economic restructuring, technological modernization, and international migration have opened up new horizons of opportunity. In view of these large-scale developments, wider society commonly rests its hope for progress and prosperity on the younger generation, which is expected to emerge as new future leaders and change agents. Persisting social, economic, and political constraints, however, obstruct young people's efforts to realize the hope for a better future life, with the result that young people seem to be increasingly unable to resolve their own difficulties, let alone the problems faced by their respective societies. The image generated through such debates is one in which youth are seen to be either the makers or the breakers of future society (Honwana and de Boeck 2005).

This discrepancy between aspirations and practicable avenues is a challenge confronted by young people across the world. In response, national governments and global institutions have developed numerous policies which seek to 'unleash' young people's capacity to act (cf. World Bank 2018). In the specific case of Nepal, the debate about young people's agency has been reinvigorated in the aftermath of a series of devastating earthquakes in 2015. Impressed by the enormous resources that educated young Nepalis were able to mobilize in a timely manner for search and rescue efforts, the media, public authorities, and international experts readily took to the idea that youth activism offered an answer to the country's lingering economic and political problems. 'Build back better' became the principal motto and Nepal's young population was called upon to look beyond immediate relief efforts and to aspire to long-term economic growth and political transformations (Hindman and Poudel 2015). Particularly in situations of adversity like this, policymakers and scholars regularly turn their attention to young people's collective actions and their potential social implications.

It is now well established among social scientists that young people have agency, but much less is known about what types of agency young people may demonstrate. My primary interest in conducting this study was, therefore, to scrutinize some of the conceptual ideas that underlie prevalent visions of youth as agents of social change and as a source of hope for a better future. In each of the empirical chapters in the book, I take up this point with reference to three vignettes of specific encounters and conversations I had with educated young Nepalis in Kathmandu. This way of retelling the stories of these young people allows for their views, experiences, and ways of being to take a central place. In line with David Arnold and Stuart H. Blackburn (2004), I suggest that these detailed accounts can reveal insights into the experiences and attitudes not just of the specific person but also of the social category of youth, more generally. I was also inspired by the work of Arnold and Blackburn (2004: 6) not least because the authors further emphasize that this way of telling people's lives 'is of particular value in seeking to understand and analyze groups that are … not normally heard'.

Basing my analysis primarily on participants' verbal accounts meant that I was required to work in two foreign languages,

Apart from students and teachers, textbooks are a significant element of educational life. The homogeneity with which we seek to build an understanding of the writing of textbooks based on religious fundamentalism alone is perhaps not the only way of looking at the problem of the textbook culture in education in India. It is equally essential to draw out other significant aspects of not only the writing of textbooks but of their transaction and impact on children's learning. This transaction depends on teachers and students and their interaction inside classrooms. It is imperative to understand these processes by focusing on children's and teachers' views on textbooks and their significance in their lives.

The volumes in the series cover a few specific themes in institutional and non-institutional contexts of educational discourse in the region: students, youth, teachers, the politics of education and citizenship, and the social, ecological, and moral issues that underlie such discourse. It is an eclectic and comprehensive approach to understanding educational activities and processes in the region as well as the spinoffs from such processes in the lives of children, youth, and teachers.

We may conclude that the series is an initiative in the discipline of sociology wherein research on education is a somewhat neglected dimension of the broader disciplinary framework in India and the rest of South Asia. As Basil Bernstein, late Karl Mannheim professor of Sociology of Education at the University of London Institute of Education, used to say, 'My dear, we're at the bottom of the pile! No one in sociology wants to study education.' Thirty years later, with marginal improvement in educational studies in sociology, this series seeks to redress this lacuna by focusing precisely on a disciplinary area that begs attention.

Meenakshi Thapan is director of Rishi Valley Education Centre, Rishi Valley, Andhra Pradesh.

Series Advisory Board

ALSO IN THIS SERIES

the study. As part of this process, I agreed with all research participants that I would protect their identity by using pseudonyms when
writing about our encounters.

The manuscript of this book has been nine years in the making and, as such, has benefited from comments I received on other
publications. Some of the empirical material presented in Chapters
3, 4, and 5 has appeared, in other guises and in part, in my articles
in *Comparative Education* (Kölbel 2013) and *Social and Cultural
Geography* (Kölbel 2018) and in my chapter, 'Nepal's Educated
Non-elite', in *Bridges, Pathways and Transitions* (Kölbel 2016). In
this book, however, I approach the material from different analytical angles and discuss it in combination with a whole set of other
narratives and findings. The book, therefore, offers a more thorough
understanding of young people's everyday life in Kathmandu and
contributes new perspectives to conceptual debates about youth,
aspiration, and mobility.

Upon completion of this book, I struggle to find the right words to
thank all those who made it possible for me to carry out, to carry on,
and to carry through this project. First and foremost, I wish to thank
the students and faculty of Patan Campus for allowing me to join
them on campus, as well as follow their daily routines, which enabled
me to learn about critical durations in their lives. I specifically would
like to acknowledge Sujata Singh and Rajju Mulmi for the excellent
research assistance they provided. I want to express my gratitude to
Linda McDowell, Craig Jeffrey, and David Gellner for their academic
guidance, and to Johanna Waters and Karen Valentin for their con-
structive feedback. I would also like to offer special thanks to Laxmi
Nath Shrestha, my language teacher, whose love for the Nepali language, his home country, and its people has been a true inspiration for
me. I thank Meenakshi Thapan and two anonymous referees for their
advice on the production of this book. I am grateful for the financial
assistance that I received from the Scatcherd Scholarship Scheme,
St Cross College, Oxford, UK, and the Economic and Social Research
Council, Swindon, UK [ES/I025073/1].

These central pillars became a solid fundament for me to build
on thanks to a number of other people who lend their support, even
though they assumed no official role in this project. I am deeply
indebted to three exceptional academics whom I look up to as my

namely, English that I already spoke fluently and Nepali that I was just about to learn. For the young Nepalis I spoke with, it was mostly the other way around. While Nepali was not necessarily the native language of all of my respondents, they all had a good command of the language and felt comfortable speaking it. Manoeuvring this linguistic challenge, however, influenced the way in which I gathered as well as worked through the data. In fact, the little Nepali textbook that I carried with me at the beginning of my field research proved to be a wonderful icebreaker. Specially those who otherwise were shy about talking to me, because they were concerned that their English-language skills did not suffice, would join me in a circle around the little booklet and help me go through the exercises and improve my pronunciation. Then again, others insisted on speaking English, even though they struggled to express their thoughts in the foreign language and could only converse in monosyllables. Having some knowledge of English is perceived to be an important marker of educational advancement and social status, particularly among the younger generation in Kathmandu (see also Liechty 2003, 2010).

In addition to considerations regarding the respondents' preferences and my own language skills, the different modes of research also influenced the use of language. I digitally recorded 50 interviews, almost half of which were in Nepali and the remaining half either in a mixture of both Nepali and English or predominantly in English. The transcripts of all the recordings were written out in English. Longer sections originally in Nepali were translated and transcribed by my research assistants. Most of the informal conversations I had with groups or individuals were originally in Nepali. When I recorded them afterwards in my research diary, I noted them down in English. As a significant share of the material was translated by my research assistants and myself—none of us being a trained translator or a native English speaker—I chose not to concentrate on respondents' use of specific concepts during data analysis. In other words, I focused more on the wider ideas that research participants sought to convey than on the exact terms they used to express themselves. In some situations, I was unable to fully account for confidentiality. Therefore, it became all the more important for me to repeatedly cross-check informed consent as I proceeded with mentors: Beatrice Fromm, whose persisting nudges and phone calls laid the foundation stone for this project; the late Colin Brock, who walked with me when the going got tough; and Joanna Pfaff-Czarnecka, who met me on the twentieth floor and saved me from dropping this book project. I am immensely thankful to Reidun Faye and Gaëtan Cousin for much-needed encouragements and for very fruitful joint writing retreats. I wish to thank Luna Shrestha Thakur and her whole family for their hospitality and for sparking my interest in the future of Nepal's younger generation. The friends I made over the course of this research process have been an invaluable source of inspiration and distraction: Rachel James, Eveliina Lyytinen, Sanne Verheul, Renate Schamböck, Sarah Schneider, Sabin Ninglekhu, Swetha Manohar, Rocio Urrutia Jalabert, Stefanie Lenk, Margaret Scarborough, Ina Zharkevich, Uma Pradhan, Marco Meyer, and the late Pratibha Khanal Tamang. Thank you all for making the nine years that I spent working towards the publication of this book in Oxford, Kathmandu, and Berlin so much more enriching and joyous.

Without the reassuring trust and love of my family, however, I may have accomplished none of this. I thank my sister for asking the right questions, in response to which I built up the confidence necessary to go ahead with this project. I thank my nieces for helping me to keep a sense of perspective regarding the important things in life. I thank my parents for giving me wings and roots and for believing in me—always.

These words of gratitude still do not suffice, for they are written exclusively in English. The best and perhaps only way to extend my gratefulness to all concerned may be for me to say: Thank you very much, *dhērai dhan'yavāda, vielen lieben Dank!*

1

Moving from Present to Future

Youth is basically the time in life when people are in search of a future.

—Anandi, 25-year-old woman, Kathmandu, November 2011

This book is a study of young people's capacity to identify and realize promising educational and occupational pathways. It is about the social influences and structuring forces that shape young people's future orientations and the uneven and often unexpected ways in which young people forge their futures. At the centre of the book are the stories of 40 young women and men who in 2011–12 were all studying, working, and living in Nepal's capital city, Kathmandu. Over the course of nine months of field research, I spoke with these young people about their educational and occupational experiences and they shared with me the aspirations and anxieties they had with regard to their own future lives. Based on these conversations, I unpack particularly critical durations in young people's lives, where the decisions they had to make with regard to their educational and occupational careers were likely to significantly shape their future life chances.

A basic premise of this book is that young people are not simply troubled victims of political and economic transformations, but active agents in their own right, capable of negotiating the structuring forces and social pressures that shape their lives (for example,

Holloway and Valentine 2000b; James, Jenks, and Prout 1998; Willis 1977; Wulff 1995). This way of framing the life experiences of young people is useful in many respects. By taking seriously young people's own ways of thinking about their situations, researchers have been able to contribute new perspectives on issues at the centre of public policy and social action, including education, employment, politics, migration, civil society, and social welfare. Increasingly, however, scholars working with young people have been called upon to move beyond what might be immediately useful in terms of policymaking and to connect with intellectual debates about the concepts and questions at the core of social scientific research (for example, Evans 2008; Hanson Thiem 2009; and Horton and Kraftl 2005, 2006). As part of this discussion, researchers have only just begun to investigate the extent to which existing conceptualizations that shape research with youth tend to reinforce stereotypical ideas attached to young people's behaviours and roles in wider society (see, for example, the debate between Roberts [2007] and Wyn and Woodman [2006, 2007]).

The principal aim of my investigations is therefore to scrutinize some of the conceptual ideas that underlie prevalent visions of youth as agents of social change and as a source of hope for a better future. Precisely because there has been, above all, a consistent theoretical concern to show that young people have agency, many scholars involved in research on young people's lives have frequently looked for instances in which young people broke with established social norms and resisted cultural hegemonies. As a result, much of the existing literature on youth assimilates young people's agency to acts of liberation, resistance, and deviance. Such a narrow perspective on youth agency, however, runs the risk of reinforcing pervasive and often polarizing depictions of youth. In order to broaden our understanding of young people's collective actions and their potential social implications, I therefore contend that it is necessary to ask: what types of agency do young people demonstrate?

In this book, I address this question with a focus on a group of young Nepalis, who have so far received comparatively little attention in both scholarly and public debates about youth in Nepal, or elsewhere, for that matter. I argue that this is precisely because their behaviour did not raise any immediate concerns about the direction in which society was moving in the future. In 2011–12, they were studying for a master's degree at a public university campus located in the Kathmandu Valley and each of them had experience of working full time alongside their university studies. All of them shared a strong desire to do well in work and study, and genuinely strove to comply with established notions of social respectability.

Born in the mid-1980s, these young people belonged to a generation of young Nepalis whose lives were forcefully shaped by political instabilities and economic uncertainties, but who, at the same time, were encouraged to aspire to higher levels of education, salaried jobs, and international migration. Despite these shared experiences, it was a highly diverse group of young Nepalis. Of the 40 research participants, 21 were women, of which seven were married and two had children at the time fieldwork was conducted. Half of them belonged to an ethnic group or a lower caste and 22 research participants had migrated to Kathmandu from various parts of the country, including some remote areas in the mountainous parts of eastern and western Nepal and in the hill region. Overall, more than half of the research participants belonged to social groups that have long been subject to forms of discrimination and are, therefore, underrepresented at university level (cf. Bhatta et al. 2008). Through my interactions with young educated Nepalis of both genders, from different social and familial backgrounds, I was not only able to unpack some changes in the established social order but could also identify which constraints still persist. This helped me to develop a more nuanced understanding of young people's agency and, specifically, of the ways in which young people's capacity to act is linked to their social and spatial identities.

My investigations into the future strategies of young people in Nepal tie into ongoing efforts to broaden the scope of youth research in ways which often challenge dominant ideas about young people's lives and help to uncover the small gestures and practices through which young people grow in their own power (see also Cole 2010; Durham 2008; Dyson 2014; Kraftl 2008). I do so by bringing the literature on youth agency into conversation with theoretical work on the concepts of aspiration and mobility. The empirical analysis presented in this book makes evident the varied nature of young people's agency and, in this way, moves beyond dualistic categorizations of youth: conformist versus deviant; aspirational versus apathetic; mobile versus immobile. The findings, therefore, are of relevance to the interdisciplinary field of youth studies, as well as to emerging debates in social scientific research and policymaking about the apparent need to produce 'aspirational citizens' and about the meanings attached to spatial (im)mobilities in contemporary societies.

In this chapter, I locate my research within the scholarly debate on the role of youth in processes of social change. More specifically, I trace important changes in the ways in which social scientists have thought about and, increasingly, worked with young people in the twentieth and twenty-first centuries. A review of more recent contributions to the field of youth studies, however, also reveals that researchers have approached questions about young people's practices from a rather narrow angle. In order to supplement this work and provide new perspectives, I want to remain particularly attentive to ideas and strategies that may be less expected given the dominant discourses on youth. For this purpose, I bring together different strands of research on the concepts of vital conjunctures, aspiration, and mobility and, in so doing, establish the theoretical foundations for my empirical analysis of young people's time–space strategies in the context of urban Nepal. Finally, I outline my research strategy and the structure and argument of the book.

Theorizing Youth and Social Change

The truism that 'youth are the future' captures very well an assumption that underlies much of the research conducted in the field of youth studies. Young people's lives are commonly perceived as critical sites through which others may gain an understanding of what the future holds (Cole and Durham 2008: 3–4). Since young people are seen to be still in the process of making their place in society, and of exploring and experimenting with different identities and options, they are thought to serve as a catalyst for social change (for example, Arnett 2000). It is through the collective decisions and actions of the younger generation that a new and different future seems to become possible. This rather hopeful conception of youth agency nevertheless directly links to public concerns about the apparent inability of young people to resolve the indeterminacies and difficulties they confront in the present. In times of political and economic crises particularly, young people often struggle to establish themselves within their respective societies and are left with a sense of being trapped in between confirmed social statuses. If youth are taken to embody the future, the problems faced by this specific subgroup of society are essentially tantamount to the dismantling of the widespread hope for future progress (Weiss 2004). Such paradoxical visions of youth whereby young people are seen to be simultaneously the makers and the breakers of future society have generated considerable debate about the social implications of young people's collective actions (Honwana and de Boeck 2005; see also Bucholtz 2002).

The theoretical foundations of the existing body of literature on youth agency can be traced back to at least as far as the beginning of the twentieth century (for example, Hall 1904). Particularly influential in this context has been the work of Karl Mannheim ([1923] 1952). In an essay published in 1923, Mannheim presented a sociological analysis of the role of the younger generation in processes of social and cultural change. He specifically drew out the problems and advantages of generational shifts. Mannheim emphasized that each generation approaches and assimilates into its socio-historical environment anew. That is, it comes into a 'fresh contact' (Mannheim [1923] 1952: 293) with the shared cultural material. As long as the norms and habits passed on by the older to the younger generation function satisfactorily, the younger generation tends to internalize these ideas unwittingly. However, at times when the established value system is no longer reconcilable with the new situation, the younger generation is likely to critically review the cultural heritage. On the one hand, this means that in the process of transmitting established social norms and cultural beliefs from one generation to the next, some of the knowledge of previous generations gets lost. On the other hand, changes in how different generations approach their social and cultural heritage are essential for a society to adjust to new structural conditions. Mannheim ([1923] 1952: 294) explicitly writes: 'The continuous emergence of new human beings ... alone makes a fresh selection possible when it becomes necessary; it facilitates re-evaluation of our inventory and teaches us both to forget that which is no longer useful and to covet that which has yet to be won.'

The idea that young people's agency emerges out of situations of friction and apprehension also resonates with Victor Turner's (1969, 1974) description of young people as liminal subjects. In anthropological thought, liminality refers to the temporary state of being situated in between confirmed social statuses—a position which raises uncertainty but also exempts from social restrictions (see also van Gennep [1909] 1960). In the liminal phase of youth, individuals are therefore seen to be uniquely poised to be highly inventive and to rethink established social norms as they are in the process of re-marking their place in society. Indeed, these early works signify a departure from previous psychobiological research into youth. Young people's experiences and practices are no longer reduced to a developmental phase in the life course between childhood and adulthood but are analysed in relation to complex processes of social change and reproduction. This conceptual move inspired researchers from across the social sciences to pay more attention to the agency of young people.

A central theme of this scholarship on young people's agency has been the significance of youth subcultures as critical sites for processes of social and cultural production. Particularly influential in this respect has been the work of researchers associated with the Centre of Contemporary Cultural Studies (CCCS), at the University of Birmingham, in the 1970s and the 1980s. The CCCS scholars, contributing to a collection of working papers titled, *Resistance through Rituals* (Hall and Jefferson 1975), argued that youth subcultures emerge within and, in fact, against the power relations around which social life is organized. With elements of Marxism forming the central theoretical pillar of a series of studies produced at the CCCS, deviance—whether in terms of certain activities, styles, or use of specific spaces—was seen as a way by which young people set themselves apart from the dominant culture and, hence, could challenge the status quo. Rather than viewing youth solely as future adults, the work of CCCS scholars made evident that young people produce something on their own that is of value for them, if not in the long term, then at least at the time. Empirically, the studies by CCCS scholars remained exclusively focused on young people's lives in post–World War II Britain. In terms of their theoretical contributions, however, the work of

CCCS scholars became a major point of reference for youth studies, directing attention to acts of rebellion and resistance, along with creativity, as hallmarks of young people's agency.

The assertion that young people's actions need to be understood as active efforts to advertise their individuality and to gain more independence is further underpinned by an extensive body of literature on young people's lives in the late twentieth and the twenty-first centuries (for example, Bynner, Chisholm, and Furlong 1997; Furlong and Cartmel 1997; Heinz 1987, 2003; Roberts, Clark, and Wallace 1994; Shanahan 2000). The burgeoning interest in youth research was spurred by public concerns over growing levels of instability and uncertainty regarding young people's transition from school to work. As a result of the economic recession in the 1980s in Europe and North America, youth unemployment rates increased significantly. At the same time, the expansion of the service industry raised expectations for educational qualifications in those countries. On the one hand, these changes in the education and labour markets allowed some young people, and especially young women, to seize on a range of new opportunities that had been largely unavailable to their parents. 'Standard biographies' specific to a person's gender and class were seen to be replaced by 'choice biographies' (for example, Brannen and Nilsen 2002; du Bois-Reymond 1998). However, young men from a working-class background seemed to lose out on these developments. Linda McDowell (2003), for example, found that the machismo and resistance associated with male working-class culture, alongside a fairly poor education, put working-class young men at a disadvantage in the changing labour market of northern England. McDowell moves on to argue that young men did not despair despite the fact that they failed to upgrade their skills and were excluded from more well-paid jobs. Rather, these young men maintained a strong dedication to hard work, which in turn enabled them to obtain relatively stable forms of employment and to build committed relationships. Taken together, these studies imply that young people's efforts to achieve independence have become more complicated, as young people can no longer rely on previously well-established pathways. Instead, they are increasingly required to construct their own routes through formal education and into the labour market, thereby drawing from a wider set of opportunities—whether by choice or not.

Human geographers and social anthropologists have further advanced this debate by contributing insights into young people's lives in other parts of the world. These studies establish that lingering political or economic crises amplify young people's struggle to map out potential future pathways. In places as diverse as Ethiopia (Mains 2012), Senegal (Ralph 2008), Papua New Guinea (Demerath 2003), and India (Jeffrey, Jeffery, and Jeffery 2008), the expansion of modern education systems coupled with a stagnant labour market has left a large number of young people without any tangible prospects for an adequate employment that would allow them to build a financially secure future. Political regulations sometimes exacerbate the struggle young people face. In the case of Rwanda, for example, the government launched a housing reform which significantly complicated young people's efforts to build a house in proximity to their rural home communities—a life achievement which is closely tied up with local notions of proper manhood (Sommers 2012). In a similar vein, young people in Lusaka, the capital city of Zambia, felt that social adulthood was beyond their grasp as they struggled to accumulate the resources necessary to move out of their parents' homes (Hansen 2005).

Whilst these studies tend to focus on male youth, the problems they outline have direct implications for young women. In many societies in Africa and South Asia, young men's financial independence is thought to be a prerequisite for obtaining a socially acceptable marriage, having children in that marriage, and providing for the family (for example, Lukose 2010; Masquelier 2005). For young women, it is particularly important to secure a favourable marriage arrangement and attain motherhood because they are likely to have even fewer opportunities to obtain other social markers of seniority, in the form of higher levels of education, professional employment, or positions of public responsibility (Stambach 2000). However, as young people's private lives become enmeshed in the uncertainties arising from daunting economic prospects and political instability, it seems impossible for young men and women alike to foresee whether and when they will be able to gain recognition as full adults. It, therefore, has been argued that societies in the Global South are faced with the imminent danger of producing 'an entire generation of failed adults', which is vulnerable to manipulation and exploitation by political forces, including militant and criminal groups (Sommers 2012: 193; see also Dore 1976; Verkaaik 2004; Vigh 2006).

Other scholars working with young people in the Global South have mitigated such ominous depictions of youth, arguing that young people may respond to unpromising circumstances in a creative, and not destructive, manner. There is now plenty of evidence to suggest that unemployed young men engage in strategic forms of waiting in order to mediate the severe lack of job opportunities (Jeffrey 2010b; Mains 2012; Newell 2012; Ralph 2008). Other studies imply that young people's resourcefulness sometimes simply resides in their ability to survive. This point emerges forcefully from Kate Swanson's (2010) account of young beggars in Ecuador. Swanson describes how young people have responded to the decline of the rural economy by migrating to the country's largest city to beg. Through begging, these young people are able to build supportive social networks and accumulate sufficient money to finance their schooling. Hannah Hoechner (2011) makes a parallel observation in her study of Qur'anic students in Nigeria. She shows that traditional Islamic education, in combination with begging or menial work in urban areas, constitutes an important coping strategy for the sons of poor rural families and enables these young men to deflect attention from the fact that they are socially excluded. The image produced by such accounts is one in which young people are seen to be highly capable of appropriating dominant structures and of negotiating situations of adversity.

Studies of youth in Nepal largely resonate with this broader debate about youth agency, with the country's younger population often being ascribed the role of society's 'change agents'. In a study of Nepali student politics, Amanda Snellinger (2005, 2009, 2018) illustrates well that youth activism is a key theme in the discourses and programmes of various, often competing, political forces, which seek to mobilize the country's young population for their own benefits. Against the backdrop of the politically tumultuous period between 2003 and 2008, Snellinger argues that youth came to be conceived of as a liminal stage. The Nepali politicians she spoke with explained that young people's 'hopes are based in tradition and aspirations of the previous generations but their flexible perspective allows them to conceive possibilities their parents did not' (Snellinger 2005: 20).

In line with this political conception of youth, the National Youth Policy, which was published in 2010 and legally enacted in 2015, depicts youth as a 'change-driving force' with the capacity to realize the political, economic, and social transformations which previous generations have not accomplished (Ministry of Youth and Sports [MoYS] 2010).

This vision of youth as a source of hope for future change also resonates with Mark Liechty's (2003: 246) description of Kathmandu's youth as the 'vanguard' of the middle-class project to construct a 'modern' future. Liechty conducted his ethnographic research in the early 1990s, when a new propertied class started to emerge in Nepal's capital city as a result of large-scale economic, political, and social transformations. These developments had direct implications for the younger population: young people's lives increasingly evolved around new social institutions—colleges, offices, clubs, shopping malls—which brought together peers of both genders and from different caste and ethnic origins. In this context, Liechty (2003: 243) argues that 'a new "in-between" domain of "youth"... opens up at the intersection of new patterns of education, labor, consumption and class formation.' Against the backdrop of structural changes transforming the country's educational and economic landscape, the English term 'youth' and the Nepali equivalent 'yuba' became less associated with the transition to adulthood than with an entirely new social category, constituting an important site for a new and different future (Liechty 2003; see also Snellinger 2013).

In practice, however, young people in Nepal seem to be mostly waiting for change to happen—be it on a personal, political, or social level (Liechty 2003; Snellinger 2009, 2010). For the established elite and the new middle class, investing in the offspring's education has come to be a question of social prestige. From the perspective of the young people themselves, however, the class-specific privilege of prolonging their education in the absence of adequate job opportunities has turned into a social dilemma. Specific markers of adulthood, such as a salaried employment and, in extension to this, a suitable marriage arrangement, are increasingly hard to achieve. Liechty (2003: 211) hence concludes that a growing number of young Nepalis are trapped 'in a kind of limbo' as they try to fulfil the hopes and dreams of middle-class families, yet without much success. A similar sense of deferment is also evident in the definitions of youth used in Nepali politics. Politicians, some of them aged 40 and above, have continued to act as 'youth leaders' because they are still waiting their turn to be promoted to the higher ranks of the party hierarchy (Snellinger 2009). Researchers working with young people in Nepal therefore broadly agree that young Nepalis are in situations of 'radical uncertainty' (Madsen and Carney 2011), as youth has emerged to be primarily a holding category for a surplus of 'adults-in-waiting' (Snellinger 2009).

The studies I have reviewed so far not only illustrate that the literature on youth agency has expanded enormously during the second half of the twentieth century and the beginning of the twenty-first century. They also epitomize the advances made in the way in which social scientists think about as well as work with young people. Perhaps most importantly, youth researchers have moved beyond narrow theories of socialization by emphasizing that young people are social agents in their own right (for example, Holloway and Valentine 2000b; James, Jenks, and Prout 1998; Willis 1977; Wulff 1995). This means that young people are no longer conceived of as passive recipients of the norms and values that adults try to pass onto them. Rather, due attention is now being paid to the perceptions of young people themselves and to the ways in which young people act upon the multitude of structuring forces and social influences that shape their lives. This conceptual move also reflects in calls for an active involvement of young people in research activities and other social processes, more generally (for example, Barker et al. 2009; Cahill 2007; Matthews, Limb, and Taylor 1999).

This significant progress notwithstanding, the visions of agency that emerge from the extensive body of literature on youth produced over the course of the past century tend to cluster around notions of youth as innovatively resourceful and a source of hope. There is, above all, a consistent concern to show how young people negotiate situations of uncertainty and adversity. In particular, attention is being directed to instances in which young people stimulate social change by breaking with established habits and beliefs and by creating new ideas and values (Ahearn 2001b; Bucholtz 2002). Youth agency is therefore commonly understood as an oppositional and inventive capacity which enables young people to assert their independence against dominant social pressures and cultural hegemonies. In some cases, theorizations of youth agency can be traced back to the rise of romanticism in the nineteenth century, and particularly to the German romantic tradition of 'storm and stress' (France 2007; see also Hall 1904). Descriptions of youth as a period of 'storm and stress' suggest that young people go through a time of rupture and crisis as they transcend childhood identities and start to build their own future lives. Over the course of the twentieth century, young people's personal growth has become increasingly linked to specific steps and achievements: completing schooling; securing a job; earning an income; and moving out of the parental home. It is commonly presumed that such accomplishments have to be achieved through an act of liberation from the familiar socio-spatial environment. From this perspective, young people's personal growth is intimately linked to social change (see Durham 2008).

Western-inspired approaches to youth agency, which emphasize the liberation of the individual as a 'self' from structuring forces, are ubiquitous both in academic writing as well as in policy discourses. However, for my work with young people in Nepal, such an understanding of youth agency is only partially useful for several reasons. First, a tight focus on individual agency draws attention away from differences in people's agency related to their social identities, including gender, caste/ethnicity, and class. In a study of poor and lower-middle-class youth in Madagascar, Jennifer Cole (2004) clearly shows that young women and men negotiate economic scarcity differently. Whilst young women could earn some money by engaging in sexual relationships with foreign visitors, young men were often left to survive through petty crime. These dynamics led to a change in local gender roles, wherein young men became increasingly reliant on their female partners and young women gained authority as the main breadwinners. Cole's study illustrates well that young people try to cope with economic difficulties based on the specific kind of agency bestowed on them by virtue of their gender identity. Jane Dyson's (2008) account of young people's involvement in lichen collection in a remote part of the Indian Himalayas is similarly helpful. Young men, especially those belonging to a lower caste, worked particularly hard in the forest as a good harvest enabled them to support their families financially. In contrast, upper-caste young women used the time in the forest for 'fun activities'. These differences in young people's work practices relate to gender norms imposed on them in more public spaces. Unlike young men, young women had few opportunities to have fun outside the forest because, in the presence of other members of the village community, it would have been socially unacceptable for young women to play games or fool around. Thus, Dyson's observations not only illustrate how gender and caste inequalities play out in young people's work practices but also highlight the spatial dimension of youth agency. In view of such findings, I suggest that more attention needs to be paid to the various ways in which young people may exercise their agency in different socio-spatial contexts as their practices are always shaped by social norms and expectations related to a person's gender, caste/ethnicity, and class.

A second difficulty with pervasive conceptualizations of youth agency from the point of view of my interest in young people's lives in Nepal is that young people's actions are generally understood as efforts to achieve greater independence in order to demonstrate maturity. In many parts of the world, however, young people's maturity and agency is measured in terms of less rather than more independence. For example, research on young people's work routines in countries in the Global South shows that young people's acceptance into adult society depends to a large extent on their ability to contribute fully to the maintenance of the household—be it in the form of domestic chores or in the form of paid labour outside the household (for example, Magazine and Sánchez 2007; Reynolds 1991). Samantha Punch (2002) makes this point explicit in her study of adult-child relations in rural Bolivia. She shows that young people were expected to accept more responsibility for their family and community as they grew up. In view of such local notions of maturity, young people's involvement in the labour market cannot only be explained by financial needs, but also by their desire to fulfil the social obligations they have towards their kin. Other studies have further contributed to this debate by directing attention to the importance of friendship ties for young people. Based on research with middle-class young men in Bangalore (today's Bengaluru), Nicholas Nisbett (2007) argues that unemployed young men were able to maintain a sense of middle-class status by sharing expensive consumer goods with their friends.

In this sense, relationships with peers are seen to open up possibilities for young people to acquire a sense of agency (see also Dyson 2010; Willis 1977). In all these contexts, young people's actions are expressions of sociality. I, therefore, propose that it is necessary to critically examine the prevalent assumption according to which young people's agency resides in their active efforts to become more independent in order to raise their social status.

This point of criticism relates to a third shortcoming, which weaves through a large share of the literature on youth agency. Starting with the work of CCCS scholars, studies of youth have been mainly concerned with deviant forms of behaviour and young people's involvement in spectacular actions. The CCCS researchers were not unaware of this limitation. In the theoretical part of their collaborative work, they note that 'the great majority of ... youth never enters a tight or coherent subculture at all' (Clarke et al. 1975: 16). Nevertheless, notions of rupture and crisis continue to be a central theme in more recent studies of youth as well, especially, though not exclusively, of young people's lives in parts of Africa and Asia. Critics have therefore noted that most youth researchers seem to have lost from sight, 'the more mundane dimensions of everyday life' for young people (Hansen 2005: 4; see also Cole 2010; Durham 2008). The majority of young people, however, remain firmly located in well-established social institutions—school, work, and family—that shape their daily lives, without necessarily questioning them. They are law-abiding, committed to doing well in school and at work, respectful of adults, and tightly connected to their families and friends (Ball, Macrae, and Maguire 2000: 93–104). Their behaviour, therefore, rarely raises any concerns about the future in which society is moving. Adults can feel reassured because the offspring appear to be in agreement with the cultural values and norms that the older generation aims to pass on to them. Precisely because 'conformist' youth are presumed to primarily reproduce the status quo, they generally receive far less attention in both scholarly and public debates (for example, Bucholtz 2002; Lave et al. 1992; Woodman 2013; Wulff 1995).

Such interpretations, however, downplay the extent to which young people may exert their power not only by resisting against dominant pressures but also by abiding by established norms. Particularly instructive in this context is Deborah Durham's (2008) research with young people in Botswana. Durham found that the young people she worked with greatly valued connections with other family members, elders, and their home communities, and actively sought to strengthen these ties. It was through their involvement in traditional social networks and their ability to listen, understand, and obey that young people learned how to 'get things done' (Durham 2008: 176), that is, how to act effectively by exercising a measure of power. Durham, therefore, emphasizes that youth researchers need to move beyond simply stating that young people have agency and, instead, need to examine more closely what kind of agency young people might have and how their agency relates them to others and to their society (Durham 2008: 153). Building on such critical contributions to the field of youth studies, I seek to develop a fuller understanding of young people's agency through my work with educated young people in urban Nepal. In particular, I aim to move beyond stereotypical ideas attached to youth by examining to what extent young people identify themselves with public discourses on the role of youth in Nepali society and with prevailing expectations about the younger population.

Vital Conjunctures of Youth

Central to the literature on youth agency are questions about young people's educational and occupational pathways. Related decisions and practices are often seen to be of major importance for people's chances of building a prosperous future life. Studies of young people's progression through the education system and into the labour market have effectively described the workings of various forces of socialization, including the family, the school, the media, and the state, to name a few (for example, Coleman 1973; James, Jenks, and Prout 1998). As a result, social scientists now broadly agree that the category of 'youth' needs to be understood as a social construction because young people's lives are always shaped by multiple dominant pressures and recursive interventions by adults (for example, Barker et al. 2009; Holloway and Valentine 2000b). Since the twentieth century, Euro-American models of how individuals should mature by completing formal schooling and entering the labour market thereafter have become manifested in people's minds across the world

(Cole and Durham 2008: 5–6; Ruddick 2003). In recent years, however, the concept of youth transitions has attracted much criticism as it assimilates young people's development to a unilinear progression through specific stages and implies that there exists a universal, normative set of behaviours and experiences through which individuals are integrated into adult society (for example, Jeffrey 2010a; Wyn and Woodman 2006, 2007). Consequently, any sort of deviance from this transitional process—whether because of young people's own actions or because of conditions beyond their control—is likely to be interpreted as a sign of a young person's inability to construct a successful future life. Whilst efforts have been made to account for non-linear transitions (for example, Hörschelmann 2011; Roberts 2007; Valentine 2003), the focus of transition literature remains on the acquisition of adulthood, that is, the end point. By contrast, I suggest that a thorough understanding of the complex and often uneven ways in which young people try to construct a future necessitates a shift in focus to the actual process of becoming. In my own analysis of the educational and occupational situations of young Nepalis, I therefore strive to adopt a contextually based approach that traces social patterns at the micro level, and hence allows me to capture heterogeneities in young people's daily practices and in their narratives about their potential future lives.

Jennifer Johnson-Hanks's (2002) theory of 'vital conjunctures' promises to be particularly useful for this purpose. Drawing from her empirical research in Cameroon, Johnson-Hanks problematizes the presumed linearity and universality of young people's life trajectories. She demonstrates that young Beti women experienced changes in their social standing linked to marriage, motherhood, employment, and formal education at different ages. Furthermore, these potentially life-changing experiences did not occur in a predictable order but sometimes took place either in parallel to each other or not at all. Johnson-Hanks, therefore, proposes a theory of 'vital conjunctures'. The term 'conjuncture' derives from the work of Pierre Bourdieu (1977) and refers to relatively short-term conditions that manifest social structure and shape the range of possible actions. With reference to young people's lives, Johnson-Hanks suggests that particular attention needs to be paid to sites of vital conjunctures when structuring elements combine in ways which make it more likely that change will happen. Such an approach takes into account the fact that a multitude of institutions forcefully shape young people's present experiences and their ideas about potential future pathways, but it also recognizes that, over time, new opportunities may open up in an often unpredictable manner and existing future orientations consequently may be re-evaluated, changed, and even reversed. Variations in young people's life experiences, then, are no longer perceived as problematic but, in fact, are to be expected, and thus are more likely to be the focus of analysis (Johnson-Hanks 2002: 878).

With the concept of 'vital conjunctures', Johnson-Hanks theoretically departs from other models which focus on specific 'turning points' (Mandelbaum 1973) or 'critical moments' (Thomson et al. 2002) around and through which people's lives evolve. She emphasizes that, as opposed to specific key events, vital conjunctures are crucial periods in people's lives which can have multiple outcomes over different time frames. Johnson-Hanks (2002: 878) explains this idea using the following example:

> Let us return now to our young man looking toward college and adult life. Instead of a liminal moment between clear and coherent stages, I suggest that his situation is a vital conjuncture. His future is largely open—up for grabs—and the alternatives that he imagines matter. The temporal coordination that he faces is the partially realized project of the social institutions that frame his alternatives, which make certain aspirations plausible, possible, or almost unthinkable.

Such a dual focus on aspirations and institutions enables a perspective towards young people's life experiences that attends to how and why their status and perceptions may change over time as they spend extensive periods in the formal education system and the labour market. In this way, the concept of vital conjunctures helps to overcome the narrow focus of transition models, which tend to be fixated on the end point of acquiring adult status. A systematic exploration of the vital conjunctures occupied by young people instead allows paying due attention to the process of 'becoming somebody' and to the whole range of potential futures under debate. Building on Johnson-Hanks's theoretical work, therefore, helps me to take better account of the multiple ways in which young people may actively reassess their own positioning and future options as they encounter persisting constraints and get exposed to new ideas and influences. Adopting a more contextually sensitive perspective, furthermore, allows me to remain attentive to changes in young people's future strategies which may be less expected based on prevalent discourses and my own assumptions. By recognizing that young people may approach the future in various ways, I suggest that it becomes possible to move away from a language of crisis and to prise open the social category of youth.

In order to do so, however, I suggest that it is necessary to explore in more depth in which situations young people are more likely to rethink and perhaps change their perceptions of self and others and, in extension to this, their own future horizons. Johnson-Hanks (2002: 872) emphasizes that 'the social analysis of a set of vital conjunctures rests on the systematic comparison of the kinds of futures the actors imagine when confronted with specific challenges.' The concept of 'aspiration', therefore, constitutes the fulcrum of an analysis of sites of vital conjunctures. Even so, Johnson-Hanks does not further specify what the concept of aspiration entails. In order to address this shortcoming, I strive to explore more fully which aspirations young people attach to their educational and occupational situations and which social influences shape their aspirations.

Moreover, I propose that a unilateral focus on temporalities risks underplaying the spatial nature of vital conjunctures. Johnson-Hanks convincingly develops the temporal dimension of the concept. She explains in detail that vital conjunctures have duration, are variable not only in pacing but also in order and synchronization. Similar to the concept of youth transitions, Johnson-Hanks's theory of vital conjunctures therefore mainly accounts for how young people develop over time. However, scholars of geography and migration studies have repeatedly shown that movements across space are equally significant for people's social status and can alter their future life chances. In an article on the geography of children and young people, Gill Valentine (2003: 38) explicitly notes that 'while children aged 5–16 should be at school, young people aged 16–25 may be at school, college or university, other forms of vocational training, in paid work, unemployed, doing voluntary work, travelling and so on. They experience far fewer spatial restrictions than their younger peers.' In line with Valentine's argument, I propose that questions about spatial mobility and immobility are a key concern for people occupying vital conjunctures of youth. A focus on young people's time–space strategies can therefore further advance our understanding of how young people experience and navigate sites of vital conjunctures.

The Politics of Aspirations

The concept of 'aspiration' has gained currency in scholarly and public debates about processes of social reproduction. In his now classic book, *Distinction* (1984), Pierre Bourdieu argues that subordinate groups tend to internalize certain limits of their social position. This can mean that people blame themselves for failing to succeed even in situations when success was very unlikely in the first place because of structural constraints beyond the individual's control. Often, however, less privileged members of society do not even aim for certain achievements that upper-status groups may take for granted, such as admission to university or a white-collar job. Rather, they develop a sense of their social limits and downscale their own future aspirations. Bourdieu refers to this internalization of comparatively low dispositions towards the future as 'the choice of the necessary'.

Expanding on this rationale, Arjun Appadurai (2004) contends that strengthening people's 'capacity to aspire' can help them to improve their lives and, in turn, can spur social transformation at a larger scale. Appadurai conceptualizes the capacity to aspire as a future-oriented form of human agency. He explicitly builds on the work of Pierre Bourdieu and other scholars who have contributed to a theory of practice (Bourdieu and Passeron 1977). Practice theorists have sought to overcome the structure/agency opposition by arguing that human actions and social structures are dialectically related and mutually reinforcing. Agency, then, never exists outside the social structure, but rather emerges from the multitude of social interactions in which people are enmeshed (for example, Ortner 2006). Appadurai (2004: 67) accounts for this dialectic by emphasizing that 'aspirations form parts of wider ethical and metaphysical ideas which derive from larger cultural norm.... They are always formed in interaction and in the thick of social life.' However, he specifically conceives of agency not only in relation to traditional values and established habits, but also as taking the form of targets, goals, future plans, hopes; in sum, aspirations.

In particular, Appadurai emphasizes that what people believe is possible for them to achieve in the future strongly influences their actions and decisions in the present. However, in order to map out potential routes to future success, information about possible destinations, shortcuts, blockages, preferable paths, and alternative ways is required. Such information is not equally available to different members of society. In line with Bourdieu, Appadurai (2004: 67–8) holds that more privileged groups are more likely to have a better understanding of a wider range of possibilities because they can resort to previous experiences of success and have sufficient resources to experiment with their ideas. Poorer members, in contrast, often struggle to construct a sufficiently detailed map to enable them to reach desired future destinations. Drawing from his ethnographical material about an alliance of slum dwellers in Mumbai, Appadurai shows that this grassroots organization provided a platform by which the urban poor could discuss and present their ideas, with the result that they were better able to identify a range of future possibilities as well as the challenges they had to tackle in order to reach their goals (Appadurai 2004: 71–80). In this way, the urban poor could advance their own agendas and become less reliant on more powerful actors, such as government authorities, private contractors, and non-governmental organizations (NGOs). Appadurai, therefore, concludes that the capacity to both set targets for the future as well as to navigate a way towards them provides a basis for upward social mobility.

The idea of raising people's aspirations in order to narrow the social gap is also reflected in discourses on policies for young people in various parts of the world. Studies in the context of the UK imply that having low aspirations for higher education and a profitable career is thought to be a deficit, which hinders children from socially marginalized or low-income families to improve their lives (Brown 2011; Crozier 2009; Raco 2009). Politics of aspiration building are therefore advocated as a way forward to raise standards of living in deprived areas and communities. In a similar vein, efforts to expand the formal education sector in countries in the Global South are commonly accompanied by public discourses on poverty reduction, economic prosperity, and social equity (for example,

Brock 2011; Little and Lewin 2011; Meinert 2009). Consequently, many young people and their families aspire to obtain educational credentials, primarily because they have come to believe that higher education offers a route to professional employment and upward mobility (for example, Dore 1976; Jeffrey, Jeffery, and Jeffery 2008; Mains 2012).

Research into the formation of young people's aspirations and potential implications for their future life chances, however, suggests that the rhetoric of hope and opportunity can be problematic. One set of studies specifically deals with the question about how young people's aspirations are shaped in social interaction and, in this context, draws attention to possible counterforces that may delimit young people's horizons of opportunity. One of the earlier accounts on this topic is a study by Burton Clark (1960), who explored how institutionalized processes shaped the educational and occupational aspirations of young people studying at junior colleges in the US. He found that students went through a sequence of procedures, including class assessments and career counselling, which led them to lower and redefine their future ambitions. Aspirations initially promoted by public discourses about equal opportunities were gently let down or 'cooled out' once students entered the higher education institution. Clark (1960: 576) concluded that 'the general result of cooling-out processes is that society can continue to encourage maximum effort without major disturbance from unfulfilled promises and expectations' (see also Goffman 1952).

More recent studies, however, indicate that socially instilled aspirations are often no longer effectively 'cooled out'. Based on his research with unemployed young men in northern India, Craig Jeffrey (2010b) shows that young men continued to uphold the hope of securing a respectable post as a civil servant, despite being acutely aware that the extraordinary number of applicants far exceeded the very few vacancies available in the government sector. Nevertheless, these young people further nurtured their career plans and continued accumulating additional educational credentials in the belief that the 'right' combination of qualifications would eventually enable them to realize their professional ambitions. Their inability to realize their aspirations, however, left these young men with a sense of disappointment, frustration, and loss.

Such anxieties are further exacerbated when young people find themselves confronted with inconsistent expectations as regards their potential futures. The work of Sarah Smith (2013) is particularly illustrative in this context. Based on her research in the disputed territories in the Indian state of Jammu and Kashmir, Smith shows that young people often found themselves torn between social expectations of modernity and the need to conform to traditional notions of social respectability. On the one hand, parents wanted their children to benefit from the new educational facilities in the urban centres which had previously remained largely inaccessible. On the other hand, sending the offspring to the city seemed to bear the risk of compromising religious identity as a result of potentially wayward romantic liaisons and lack of supervision. Parents' attempts to guide their children towards a desired 'modern' future and, simultaneously, impose their parental authority on young people's mobility put the young generation in a state of uncertainty and disorientation, or, in Smith's words, a 'generational vertigo'.

These studies show that a host of social and institutional actors, such as parents, peers, education professionals, mass media, and policymakers, try to influence young people in their attempts to move towards a desirable future. Through this kind of forward projection of young people's lives and behaviours, others try to develop a sense of what the future may hold. From the perspective of the younger generation, however, it is difficult to negotiate these diverse and often incompatible visions of potential futures. Consequently, youth appear to be particularly affected by the high levels of uncertainty inherent in the future, and even more so when the futures they are encouraged to envision stand in stark contrast with the realities of their present-day lives. The gap that exists between encouragements to achieve and actual chance of realizing achievement is a problematic one, as it tends to leave individuals with a sense of disappointment and failure. Some scholars have even warned that such heightened levels of frustration among the younger population bear the risk of social unrest (for example, Dore 1976; Sommers 2012).

Discrepancies between young people's aspirations and their chances of realizing these aspirations prompt further questions about the specific content and nature of socially instilled future orientations. Sarah Holloway and Helena Pimlott-Wilson (2011), for example, raise the question about what defines parental aspirations for their children as low. In interviews with education practitioners in the UK, it became apparent that efforts to widen children's horizons of opportunity largely evolved around the valorization of academic education and a professional career. However, setting such norms about the kind of aspirations perceived to be 'appropriate' generally neglects alternative ideas of happiness and well-being, and even downgrades certain other achievements in life, such as founding a family and taking responsibility as a parent. More importantly, judgements about what constitutes 'appropriate' future aspirations tend to be made against established middle-class standards (Holloway and Pimlott-Wilson 2011; see also Raco 2009). Nitya Rao's (2010) study of young people's educational and occupational aspirations in a rural community in eastern India is similarly compelling. Her observations complicate developmental discourses proclaiming that hopes for a greater degree of personal and financial autonomy are the reasons behind the increase in girls' enrolment rates. Most Hindu parents are willing to invest in their daughters' education not because they want their daughters to become more self-reliant, but because upper-status men increasingly prefer their wives to be well educated (see also Donner 2005). These studies indicate that young people's aspirations may not necessarily provide a potential map for upward social mobility, but may as well reflect and reinforce established social hierarchies of class, gender, and caste/ethnicity.

In order to avoid reproducing normative discourses about young people's potential futures in academia, attempts have been made to call more attention to young people' own articulations of hope (for example, Bishop and Willis 2014; Pain et al. 2010). By contrasting representations of childhood and hope in policy reports with young people's own narratives, Peter Kraftl (2008) has developed a particularly nuanced and politically aware understanding of young people's modes of hoping. Kraftl found that policymakers and charities working on behalf of children intimately link childhood to notions of hope and futurity in an often universalizing and simplistic manner. In comparison, children's ways of hoping are far less spectacular than such adult-constructed representations suggest. Kraftl (2008: 88) further specifies that 'hope was manifested in very small steps, relatively *modest* coping mechanisms and minute changes in individuals' attitudes to life. Through these, diverse fragments of hope may be allowed to foment, small opportunities may begin to present themselves.' In order to interrogate more modest forms of hoping, Kraftl suggests that we should not simply replace 'high-profile' representations of childhood and hope with more 'low-key' forms of hoping. Rather, research into young people's future orientations needs to critically review dominant discourses about youth and futurity by developing a reinvigorated understanding of how hope is figured through young people's everyday practices and routines.

To summarize, the idea of raising people's aspirations to help them improve their lives has generated considerable controversy. I take from Appadurai's (2004) theoretical work that an exploration of young people's future horizons can reveal much about why young people try to seize on particular opportunities in the present. By considering which new information and additional experiences they may gather over time and across space, it also becomes possible to understand why some future plans become more concretized, while others may need to be revised or dropped altogether. A future-oriented approach to young people's behaviours and actions can, therefore, provide new insights into how young people navigate their social spaces (Appadurai 2004: 84). However, an uncritical emphasis on young people's capacity to plan for alternative futures and identify ways to move towards them runs the risk of reproducing prevailing notions of youth as 'change agents' and of downplaying the extent to which young people's lives are deeply embedded within established social structures. Existing research on the formation of young people's aspirations points towards a whole range of possible counterforces which may delimit young people's aspirations or may severely complicate the realization of their aspirations. Consequently, I hold that young people's chances of realizing socially instilled future ideals are not solely a matter of their capacity to aspire, but also need to be understood within the context of wider social, economic, and political circumstances. In this book, I therefore look more closely at both the content of young people's aspirations and the extent to which their aspirations correspond to their social and economic opportunities. Moreover, I am interested in finding out to what extent young people identify with dominant discourses on the role of youth in future society. In so doing, I strive to remain critical of the politics involved in the formation of young people's aspirations and attentive to alternative and perhaps more subtle ways of figuring the future.

Young People's (Im)mobilities

Movement has been the subject of investigation throughout the history of the discipline of geography and related subfields, especially migration studies. Researchers contributing to this literature have effectively described certain patterns of human mobility, such as international versus internal migration, skilled versus unskilled migration, or temporary versus permanent migration. In this way, they have identified a range of motivations for people to migrate and have disclosed diverse experiences of migrants at either end of the relocation process. More importantly, migration experts have shown that human mobility has come to play a vital role in reshaping societies and politics around the world (for example, Castles and Miller 2009). It appears to be increasingly necessary for people to move in order to earn a living, to find a safe place to stay, to obtain an education, and to reunite with family and friends. In this sense, mobility is seen to constitute an essential resource for people to make a living and, more generally, for the functioning of society. As a result, questions about the implications of the growing magnitude and significance of human mobility for individual actors and for society at large have gained in urgency in social science research.

In response, researchers from across the social sciences have called for a 'new mobilities paradigm'. In particular, it has been argued that there is a need to move beyond primarily documenting how human mobility has intensified both in pace and in scope. More importantly, scholars need to examine how social life can be re-thought through mobility rather than stasis and structure (see Sheller and Urry 2006). Recent contributions to mobilities research seek to do so by unpacking the complex ways in which different forms of mobility are interrelated to one another and connected across different scales. Due to technological innovations and global trade relations, foreign places and cultural plurality have become an integral part of people's everyday life across the world (for example, Salazar 2011). Even those individuals who are physically settled can now explore distant places by travelling through the virtual space. Consequently, people's mobility practices are no longer only a matter of physical movement per se, but need to be understood within the context of a variety of things moving—be it other people, ideas, or objects. Within the mobilities paradigm, scholars therefore seek to foreground mobility as a geographical fact that lies at the centre of the micro-geographies of everyday life (Cresswell 2010).

By making mobility the focal point of analysis, mobilities research theoretically departs from existing studies of human mobility. Previously, research into people's movements has been primarily concerned with pre- and post-migration experiences, that is, with the end points of the migration process. Within the mobilities paradigm, by contrast, movement is no longer taken for granted as a connection between two locations but constitutes the very subject of enquiry. Re-approaching mobility in this way has several outcomes, as Tim Cresswell (2006: 265) specifies:

> In this world it is important to understand that mobility is more than about just getting from A to B. It is about the contested world of meaning and power. It is about mobilities rubbing up against each other and causing friction. It is about a new hierarchy based on the ways we move and the meanings these movements have been given.

As emphasized by Cresswell (2006), mobility is rarely a neutral act; it is always filled with meaning. Mobility has no pre-existing significance in and of itself; it is not essentially good or bad. Rather, mobility is read and interpreted against established societal norms and value systems, which may or may not be specific to a particular place and a particular time. Furthermore, the meanings given to mobility are intimately connected to the different ways in which people practise, experience, and embody mobility. Cresswell, therefore, contends that it is essential for mobilities scholars to attend to the specific context in which mobility takes place and to the distinct ways in which social actors are positioned in relation to flows and interconnections. Without due attention to the social and experiential dimensions of mobility, Cresswell argues, academic work would ignore that mobility is of political significance in contemporary societies, and hence would fail to capture the complex relationship between spatial mobility and social mobility.

The idea that there is more to mobility than mere movement also resonates with Doreen Massey's (1993) formulation of a 'power-geometry'. Massey is particularly critical of the prevalent impression that as long as people have sufficient money, they can take equal advantage of mobility in contemporary societies. By contrast, she holds that mobilities are unevenly experienced in relation to a whole range of markers of social difference, including gender, age, class, ethnicity, nationality, and geographical origin. Accordingly, differences in people's access to certain kinds and qualities of mobility tend to reflect already existing social inequalities and hierarchies. Massey moves on to argue that those individuals or social groups with better access to mobility may use their mobility to reinforce and improve their social standing. She writes: 'It is not simply a question of unequal distribution, that some people move more than others, some have more control than others. It is that the mobility and control of some groups can actively weaken other people' (Massey 1993: 62). Thus, the key point of Massey's argument about the 'power-geometry' inherent in mobility is much more than the recognition that mobility is socially differentiated. Rather, she emphasizes that mobilities can reproduce existing inequalities and may even lead to new forms of social differentiation.

Taken together, such interventions imply that an increase in mobilities does not displace or replace immobilities. As other key contributors to mobilities research assert, 'there is no linear increase in fluidity without extensive systems of immobility' (Hannam, Sheller, and Urry 2006: 3). Accordingly, mobility and immobility must not be thought of as mutually exclusive; on the contrary, the mobility of some individuals is inevitably linked to the immobility of others. To some extent, the relationship between mobility and immobility is a question of who initiates and controls mobility and who is controlled or even imprisoned by it (see Massey 1993). However, research has also shown that some individuals strategically choose to remain rooted in place in order to facilitate and sustain the mobilities of others. The work of migration experts is particularly instructive in this context, as it shows that non-movers play an active role in migration processes (for example, Cohen and Sirkeci 2011: 87–96; Goldin, Cameron, and Balarajan 2011: 179–93). Those who stay at home serve as an important connection that anchors and secures the migrant. Sometimes, non-movers even initiate mobility practices by providing the financial means required by others to become spatially mobile in the first place. Such accounts challenge pervasive associations based on which immobility increasingly acquires the connotation of passiveness, failure, backwardness, and social exclusion and urge for further in-depth investigations into the relationship between mobilities and immobilities.

Geographical work on children and youth reveals that questions about spatial mobility and immobility are a key concern, especially for young people (for example, Barker et al. 2009; Geisen 2010; Holloway and Jöns 2012; Smith, Rérat, and Sage 2014). Of particular relevance in this context are studies concerned with the growing significance of spatial mobilities for young people's learning and education. As the common expression 'going away to uni' exemplifies, the association between young people's spatial mobility and higher levels of education has become deeply manifested in the social consciousness (Holdsworth 2009). More recently, however, the presumed connection between enhanced levels of spatial mobility and educational attainment seems to have reached an entirely new scale in view of the unprecedented number of international students attending universities outside their home countries. In particular, a 'Western' education has become associated with a whole range of benefits, including advanced language skills, improved intercultural competencies, and a higher degree of self-reliance and flexibility (Brooks and Waters 2011: 150–1; for example, Hannerz 1996). As more young people obtain university degrees, these additional experiences and qualifications are seen to provide a competitive advantage in the local job market (for example, Brown, Hesketh, and Williams 2003; Waters 2009). Such findings imply that decisions on student mobility need to be understood within the context of young people's 'life planning' and their long-term prospects for a profitable career and a successful future life (Brooks and Everett 2008; Findlay et al. 2012).

The increase in educational opportunities and related mobility practices has not only implications for young people's future orientations but also for society at large. Geographical research shows that education-related mobilities often reflect patterns of social segregation. Based on statistical data available on the enrolments and performance of secondary schools in London, geographers have demonstrated that the best-performing schools tend to attract students from a wider area and from richer neighbourhoods (Butler et al. 2007; Hamnett and Butler 2011; Harris 2013). Such findings imply that more privileged social groups are better able than others to lay propitious foundations for their children's future, mainly because they can draw on the cultural, social, and economic resources necessary to navigate an increasingly complex education market. Research into the internationalization of higher education further suggests that such strategies of social reproduction are more and more played out at the global level (Findlay et al. 2012; Xiang and Shen 2009). Johanna Waters's (2006, 2012) research on student mobilities between Hong Kong and Canada is particularly instructive in this context. Waters shows that the benefits associated with an international education are almost exclusively available to upper-class families, who can afford to send their children abroad to study in North America. While children from lower social classes are also increasingly well educated, they primarily rely on the education provided locally. Waters (2006: 1046), therefore, argues that 'international education is transforming the spatial scales over which social reproduction is achieved.'

The global upward trend in international student migration is seen to perpetuate hierarchies not only within societies but also between regions and nations. Research on the internationalization of tertiary education reveals that higher education institutions are primarily judged based on their national identity, whilst their distinct institutional identities are often of secondary importance (Marginson and van der Wende 2007). This becomes particularly apparent with regard to the high appreciation of Western anglophone education in various parts of the world, and specifically in the Asian context (Brooks and Waters 2011). This general trend has been linked to the historically strong influence of colonial powers and foreign aid on the national education systems of countries in the Global South (Madge, Raghuram, and Noxolo 2009; Rizvi 2000). More recently, global rankings in higher education continue to reinforce the significance of a 'Western' education as a form of symbolic capital (Findlay et al. 2012; Marginson and van der Wende 2007). The implied global hierarchy in higher education and related imagined geographies have implications for the power relations that underpin the global knowledge system. On the one hand, anglophone countries are able to manifest their leading position at the international level. On the other hand, major 'sending' countries, among them China, South Korea, and India (Goldin, Cameron, and Balarajan 2011: 122), also play an important role in the global education market. Whether from the perspective of the demand side or the supply side, international student migration constitutes a key concern for multiple stakeholders, who either try to profit from this global trend or attempt to control and restrict students' mobilities (Altbach and Knight 2007; Brooks and Waters 2011: 22–44).

In view of these developments, some authors have argued that most countries in the Global South are being placed at the periphery (Altbach 1989). However, shifting the focus to these countries may, in fact, contribute to a fuller understanding of young people's mobilities and related social effects. Studies conducted in the Global South have been particularly successful in challenging the assumption that institutions within the formal education system are the primary loci of knowledge acquisition (Froerer and Portisch 2012; see also Holloway et al. 2010). Instead, they demonstrate that young people's learning takes place in various spaces around which their daily lives are organized. The connection between young people's spatial mobility, learning processes, and livelihood strategies has been made explicit by Filippo Osella and Caroline Osella (2000). Based on their field research in Kerala, south India, the authors show that labour migration to countries in the Gulf region constitutes a vital opportunity for young men to earn money, to see a new place, to acquire new skills, and to accumulate consumer goods. The newly gained wealth and experiences, in turn, allow these young men to attain social recognition as mature men who can provide for their families and the wider community. The authors, therefore, conclude that 'Gulf migration has begun to play a crucial role in movements along the male life-cycle' (Osella and Osella 2000: 120).

These findings underpin the assertion that it is difficult, and perhaps even counterproductive, to make a sharp distinction between education and labour migration. Migrating for work purposes— whether within or across national borders—entails a variety of learning processes in the form of new technical and social skills, the acquisition of a foreign language, or the very experience of travelling to an unfamiliar place and assimilating to a different lifestyle (Parry 2003; Rao and Hossain 2012). Similarly, young people's decision to migrate for educational purposes often forms an integral part of their occupational careers, as many young migrants work alongside formal education out of immediate financial needs or because of more long-term interests in economic opportunities that are unavailable or severely limited back home (Olwig and Valentin 2015; Valentin 2012b). This suggests that it is important to think through young people's mobilities in broader terms than the distinction between education and labour migration suggests and to explore how different forms of mobilities link to the ultimate aim to 'make a living' in an increasingly interconnected world (Sørensen and Olwig 2002).

Whilst the hope for improved living standards motivates many young people to relocate to a new place, it is not at all certain that spatial mobility indeed leads to social ascent. Research conducted in India (Cross 2010) and Kenya (Frederiksen 2002) shows that many young people decide to move from rural areas to the city because they want to find an employment that matches their educational attainments. However, young migrants often come to realize that the education they have obtained back home is of little value within the urban context. Faced with a highly competitive urban labour market, many young migrants are therefore confronted with a sense of disillusion and sometimes with severe economic problems. In a similar vein, studies conducted in anglophone countries reveal that the influx of international student migrants is often viewed with scepticism by the local population and, in the worst case, has exacerbated forms of discrimination based on young people's national or racial backgrounds (Collins 2010). In addition, institutional practices and stricter immigration laws further limit opportunities for migrants to integrate into the host community (Fincher and Shaw 2009; Madge, Raghuram, and Noxolo 2015). Rather than being able to fulfil the hope for a better future life, young migrants may find themselves exposed to numerous risks and to the prospect of their own future marginality as a result of moving to an unfamiliar place.

In public discourses, however, negative implications of spatial mobility are often represented in a rather one-dimensional manner, in the sense that they tend to be associated with specific purposes of migration and even specific destinations. Laura Kunreuther (2006), for example, found that the stories of foreign workers in the Gulf region broadcasted on the radio in the home country fuel anxieties about horrific work conditions, exploitation, and discrimination. In comparison, Francis Collins's (2012) research on the Internet as an important source of information for young people interested in studying abroad shows that the ideas and images disseminated about educational opportunities and student life in New Zealand paint a rather idealistic picture. In a similar vein, it has been argued that the dominant images and discourses of foreign places tend to be directional, as they commonly imply that the 'urban' or the 'West' are more advanced, wealthy, sophisticated, or simply better than the 'rural' or the 'East' (Madge, Raghuram, and Noxolo 2009; Vanderbeck and Dunkley 2003). These studies put into perspective the assertion that technological advancements, and especially the proliferation of online media, can facilitate cultural exchanges and open up new opportunities for an enhanced mutual understanding (Adams and Ghose 2003; Holloway and Valentine 2000a). As mass-mediated associations are hardly value-free, it is likely that they further implant stereotypical ideas based on which young people's mobility practices are being judged by others. In addition, these accounts indicate that, in an interconnected world, it is necessary to understand young people's perceptions and related future orientations in the context of both observable practices and imagined geographies. Fazal Rizvi (2011: 697–8) emphasizes this point in writings on student mobility in that he notes:

> As people—as well as governments and institutions such as universities—experience on a daily basis the realities of transnational economic relations, technological and media innovations, and cultural flows that cut across national borders, with greater speed and intensity than ever before, they increasingly use these experiences to make strategic calculations of their futures, and how they might take advantage of the opportunities global interconnectivity now offers. These calculations are not however made in a void, but within an imaginary of global conditions and possibilities.

As this quote exemplifies, it is now generally recognized that enhanced levels of mobility and global connectivity equally affect those young people actively involved in travels as well as those of their peers who are relatively settled in one place. Nonetheless, it can be criticized that the relevant literature has been primarily focused on the question, 'why young people move', but has neglected the twin question, 'why some of them do not move' (Hammer and Tamas 1997; see also Fortier 2014). There are a few exceptions to this general trend, however. Peter Fischer and Gunnar Malmberg (2001), for example, analysed age-specific migration patterns in Sweden and found that some people are strongly committed to a certain place because they are deeply embedded in the local community or because they are in a stable employment situation. Such factors contribute to a sense of rootedness, as a result of which people are likely to continue residing in a specific location throughout their lives. Fischer and Malmberg (2001) emphasize that people may consciously decide to stay in one place in order to seize upon 'location-specific insider advantages'. More recently, Johanna Waters and Maggi Leung (2013, 2014) conducted a study on new degree programmes offered by British universities in Hong Kong. These programmes present an alternative educational pathway to those young people who could neither secure a place in one of the domestic universities nor afford to study abroad. In particular, the students appreciated that these new educational opportunities were generally less expensive, required less time for completion, and offered more flexibility for young people already in employment. These accounts imply that relative immobility may, in fact, offer a number of benefits. However, a unilateral focus on mobility tends to see the reasons for immobility primarily in the risks involved in moving to a new place and, hence, may reproduce the misleading impression that spatial immobility is self-evidently a form of passiveness and increasingly an obstacle to social mobility.

In order to avoid such an oversimplification of the relationship between spatial mobility and social mobility, I seek to address two interrelated questions: why do some young people move and why do others stay in one locality? In this context, I interrogate young people's spatial practices across various scales, ranging from mass migration movements over virtual travels using online social media to small-scale mobilities which form part of young people's daily routines. In so doing, I not only account for the fact that young people are actively engaged in different forms of mobilities and relative immobilities, but I also want to gain a fuller understanding of how their perceptions of self and others and their future orientations relate to dominant representations of spatial mobilities. In particular, I aim to further unpack what meanings are given to young people's (im)mobilities and how certain spatial practices influence young people's potential to become socially mobile. In this way, I hope to contribute not only to studies of the geography of youth but also, more generally, to mobilities research.

Organization of the Book

This book uses a focus on young people's mobility practices and future orientations in the context of their educational and occupational experiences to engage with conceptual debates about youth, aspiration, and mobility. A central aim is to unpack the complexity of the concept of agency through a close examination of the ways in which young people align heightened aspirations for a new and different future with the often incompatible realities of present-day life. I argue that young people in urban Nepal did not develop a sense of agency primarily by asserting their own individuality and by opposing social norms; instead, they were careful to consider how others might be affected by their decisions as they strove to fulfil social obligations and foster strong relationships. By documenting how young people juggled the competing responsibilities of education, work, and family, I offer a way to rethink young people's role in processes of social change that can better account for the uneven and often unexpected ways in which young people forge futures (see also Johnson-Hanks 2002).

Adopting a future-oriented approach to an analysis of young people's agency proves to be particularly useful in this context. I argue that expressions of youth agency may not only take the form of practices as they are performed and observed in the present. Thinking ahead and anticipating the consequences of one's own actions were likewise seen to be important virtues that allowed a young person to gain social respect and to build a successful future life. At the same time, I show that it is important to verify to what extent encouragements to succeed tally with the economic and social opportunities available to young people. More than Appadurai (2004) did in his research into the future-orientated strategies of slum dwellers in Mumbai, I attend to a range of possible counterforces which may obstruct young people's attempts to live up to social expectations for the educated younger generation. In particular, I trace how social pressures linked to gender, caste/ethnic, class, and spatial identities influenced young people's chances of realizing their aspirations. By attending to how young people talked about and negotiated important decision-making situations in which potential futures were under debate, I contribute to a better understanding of young people's capacity to act upon the world reflexively, yet without neglecting to observe the limits to young people's agency posed by social hierarchies and structural constraints.

The book also highlights the importance of different forms of spatial mobility and relative immobility for young people's attempts to negotiate social pressures and develop self-images as competent, educated, and successful people. I show that education-related mobilities—be they in the form of the daily commute to the campus, the move to the capital city, or the prospect of studying abroad—served as ways in which young people distinguished themselves from the parental generation and their less educated peers. However, by asking not only 'why some people moved' but also 'why others did not', I problematize widespread perceptions according to which spatial mobility is increasingly seen to be the preferred option. I show that, in some cases, young people were able to accumulate relevant cultural and social resources precisely because they chose to stay and remain rooted in their home communities. Such findings help scholars grasp young people's capacity to navigate an increasingly interconnected world and contribute to a better understanding of the complex relationship between spatial (im)mobilities and social ascent, more broadly.

In the next chapter of this book (Chapter 2), I situate the lives of Nepalis born in the 1980s within the history of the modern Nepali state and its ties to regional and global developments. Drawing on existing literature on Nepal, I show that the newly educated young generation was seen to be particularly well prepared to take advantage of a range of new opportunities associated with educational expansion and international migration. Yet, these large-scale structural changes also caused much uncertainty, since long-established life paths seemed increasingly irrelevant, or at least more obscured. Educated young Nepalis, therefore, often struggle to reconcile pervasive discourses about a better future with the realities of their present-day lives in Kathmandu. In this context, I show that the relevant debate about the agency of youth continues to revolve around dualistic categorizations, not least because it remains focused on specific subgroups of youth, and especially on educated young men who are involved in more spectacular actions. With the aim to broaden our understanding of young people's agency, I therefore sought to work with a more heterogeneous group of university students.

Chapters 3, 4, and 5 present the empirical findings of the research, each structured in a way to approach students' educational and occupational pathways from three different angles. The subsequent discussion makes apparent that, when read together, these three different perspectives help to develop a nuanced understanding of young people's capacity to forge a future for themselves and their families.

In Chapter 3, I investigate the potential and limitations that educated young Nepalis associated with their university studies. Changes in the composition of the student body indicate that a growing number of students from social groups previously not represented at university now obtain academic credentials. Their participation in higher education gives reason to hope for a more socially just and prosperous future. In order to take full advantage of newly emerging educational opportunities, young people often felt compelled to relocate to the capital city or to go abroad. Certain educational or occupational pathways associated with an upper social status, however, remained out of reach for the majority of these students. Through an analysis of the students' educational trajectories and related future orientations, I identify which social influences most powerfully shaped young people's lives and, in so doing, critically engage with the concept the 'capacity to aspire'.

In Chapter 4, I examine to what extent the students I worked with identified with somewhat stereotypical images projected onto the university campus and explain how students tried to negotiate numerous competing social pressures on an everyday basis. In an effort to comply with established notions of female and male respectability, the students made use of the campus in different and often unexpected ways. In this regard, it proved to be useful to think through the decisions that students made in relation to their university studies as sites of vital conjunctures. This conceptual approach makes it possible to appreciate the various ways in which young people develop a sense of agency without neglecting the significant extent to which young people's educational experiences are shaped by pervasive social norms and persisting structural constraints. In shifting the focus of the analysis onto the reasons behind students' absence from and presence on campus, I call attention to the spatial dimension of young people's agency and, in so doing, advance our conceptual understanding of vital conjunctures of youth.

In Chapter 5, I move away from the campus and explore how educated young people tried to align heightened aspirations for a financially secure future with the realities of their present-day occupational situations. I show that the students were acutely aware of the difficulties involved in their attempts to carve out lucrative careers and to gain recognition for the educational credentials they obtained from a public university campus. I argue that public debates about the role of educated youth in Nepali society were part of this problem, as they tended to reinforce polarizing depictions of youth as the panacea for and a menace to the prosperous future Nepali society longed for. Precisely because my respondents' efforts to 'do good' were much more low-key than dominant representations of youth suggest, the contributions these young people made to the wider social good were largely overlooked. I show, however, that modest appropriations of dominant educational and occupational strategies allowed these young people to develop a sense of themselves as competent people and enabled them to maintain generally positive outlooks on life. These findings mitigate the language of crisis characteristic of recent scholarly and public debates about young people's capacity to act in and upon the world effectively.

Chapter 6, finally, connects the empirical analysis back to broader conceptual debates about youth, aspiration, and mobility, and thus highlights the relevance of my research with a group of young people largely overlooked by scholars and policymakers. Through an in-depth analysis of young people's time–space strategies and their current positions within existing socio-spatial hierarchies, this book develops an understanding of young people's expressions of agency in such a way as to move beyond restrictive stereotypes. It also provides new perspectives on the limitations and the potential of politics of aspiration building and throws light on the significance of spatial (im)mobility for people's life chances.

2

Preparing for the Future

A review of the origins of the field of youth studies reveals that some of the limitations of existing conceptualizations of youth agency can be ascribed to methodological issues. Until the 1990s, empirical studies of youth dealt almost exclusively with urban, white young men and were primarily conducted in countries in the Global North. While the body of literature on young people's lives in countries in South Asia and, more generally, in the Global South has expanded rapidly since the beginning of the twenty-first century (for example, Cole 2004; Dyson 2014; Jeffrey 2010b; Lukose 2010; Mains 2012), a large share of the empirical work is still focused on specific sub-groups of youth, especially young people who are either at risk of marginalization or involved in spectacular actions.

In a similar vein, researchers working in Nepal first became interested in young people's lives in the face of large-scale social and political changes (for example, Ahearn 2001a; Hirslund 2012; Liechty 2003; Skinner 1990; Snellinger 2018; Valentin 2005; Zharkevich 2009). Through the lens of the lived experiences of a generation of Nepalis born in the 1970s and 1980s, these studies shed light on one of the most turbulent times in the country's history. During this period, Nepali society witnessed the downfall of the autocratic monarchy and the re-establishment of a multiparty democracy under a constitutional monarchy in 1990. After 1996, the country was plunged into a decade-long civil war, which resulted in the abolition of the monarchy and the announcement of a republic in 2008. The Constituent Assembly, elected in 2008, however, failed to reach consensus on the structure of the federal government despite four extensions and repeated delays and, eventually, was dissolved in May 2012, shortly after I had completed my field research in Kathmandu. In an effort to develop a better understanding of these large-scale political transformations and their social implications, existing studies of youth in Nepal have been primarily concerned with young people's deviant behaviour and their involvement in acts of resistance against the established social order and the country's political system.

These changes in the political space have also significantly affected the country's educational and economic landscape. Over the course of three decades, the formal education sector has expanded in a rather uncontrolled manner. A rapid increase in gross enrolment rates at post-secondary school level from a mere 5 per cent in 2003–4 (Central Bureau of Statistics [CBS] 2004: 76) to 17 per cent in 2010–11 (CBS 2011: 96) gives reason to hope that formal education has become accessible to larger sections of Nepali society. However, particularly within the urban Kathmandu Valley where gross enrolment rates at the tertiary level have been reported to be even as high as 66 per cent in recent years, the privatization of educational provision has consolidated the role of formal education as a marker of social difference and spatial disparities (Caddell 2006; Kölbel 2017). At the same time, new technologies, such as mobile phones and the Internet, have entered the daily lives of Kathmandu's urban society, offering new means to connect to the outside world. Long-distance migration has become an important livelihood strategy of Nepalis from across the society. These developments tend to raise hopes for a new and different future, but they also cause much uncertainty as long-established life paths seem to no longer provide reliable points of reference.

In this chapter, I take a closer look at the emergence of the social category of youth against the backdrop of large-scale transformations witnessed by Nepali society during the second half of the twentieth century. Drawing on existing literature on Nepal, I trace how the expansion of the country's higher education sector and a trend towards foreign migration led to the manifestation of a specific idea of what it means to be a part of the country's educated youth—in terms of both social privileges and obligations. My analysis shows that representations of youth prevalent in the public rhetoric in Nepal are influenced to a significant degree by the practices of educated young men belonging to upper-status groups. With the aim to complement existing research, I therefore sought to engage with a heterogeneous group of young Nepalis with regard to established markers of social difference—be it gender, caste/ethnicity, class, or geographical origin. In this way, my research into the future strategies of young people in Nepal ties in with ongoing efforts to broaden the scope of youth research and, in turn, to develop a more comprehensive understanding of the concept of agency.

The Production of Educated Youth

One of the first images that captured my attention when I arrived in Kathmandu in September 2011 was a large, colourful piece of graffiti painted on a long cement wall adjoining one of the city's busiest roads. Life-size capital letters read in English, 'we make the nation'. Each letter was filled with images and messages associated with a hopeful future, often emphasizing values attached to education, unity, economic growth, and peace. Additional investigations revealed that this street art was created by a crowd of young people who had followed a call for initiative by two Nepali visual artists, both in their mid-twenties. By painting the wall with colourful and positive images, these two young Nepalis and their helpers sought to make a counterstatement to the many political slogans which otherwise dominated the public space in the city. In an interview published in a local youth magazine, one of the project conveners declared: 'Wherever we go, politicians have taken over the walls of the city. You see slogans, posters, and symbols everywhere.... This is an effort to wake up everyone in the nation to start taking responsibility' (Ghale 2011). However, it did not take long for the public space to be reclaimed by precisely those politically motivated messages. When I walked past the same wall again a few weeks later, I discovered that it had been whitewashed and painted over with big scarlet letters in Nepali, announcing a national meeting of one of the major political parties. Other posters and party emblems of political rivals had already been plastered over it and partly ripped off again, making the wall look somewhat shabby and tattered.

The wall and its record of paintings can be understood as a projection screen of the most prevalent images commonly attached to educated youth in Kathmandu. On the one hand, youthful activism is seen to provide a potential answer to the many challenges Nepali society continues to face. On the other hand, young people's active involvement in party politics tends to raise concerns which are in opposition to more hopeful perceptions of youth. Such polarized conceptions of youth agency are, of course, not specific to the case of Nepal (Honwana and de Boeck 2005), nor are they necessarily new (Majupuria and Majupuria 1985). However, such contradictory images of youth as the makers or breakers of future society still forcefully influence how Nepal's youth in general, and public university students in particular, are represented in public and scholarly debates.

This is despite of the fact that the term 'youth' (*yuba*) only gained currency in political and developmental discourses during the second half of twentieth century. Previously, there was less of a sense that the life cycle was arranged around distinct developmental stages. In most Nepali communities, it was common for children to accept responsibilities associated with adulthood at an early age, especially where people's livelihoods depended on subsistence farming (Bista 1991: 69; see also Dyson 2014). Only the upper castes, namely, Brahmin, Chhetri, and some Newar Hindus, had long distinguished between children and adults. In the tradition of these communities, male and female initiation rituals were seen to mark a young person's transition to adulthood and acceptance as a full member of the community (Bennett 1983). Whilst such ceremonies are still performed in Nepal to date and perhaps have even gained in importance as a stage to demonstrate the family's social status, they have little to do with the construction of youth as a social category in contemporary Nepal (Michaels 2004: 98–9). In the case of Nepal, the social construct of youth therefore constitutes a modern concept, one which cannot be directly linked to any of the multiple cultural traditions found within Nepal (see also Snellinger 2013).

In particular, the rapid expansion of the formal education sector during the second half of the twentieth century gave rise to new social categories, according to which the 'educated' youth was to be distinguished from the 'uneducated' older generation (Kölbel 2013; Skinner and Holland 1996; Valentin 2005). This distinction was fed by the strong belief that modern schooling equips a person with more than literacy and numeracy skills: schools and colleges represent crucial sites for the formation of values and attitudes, and teach young people about the role they are expected to play in future society. In this context, researchers working with university students in Nepal—and elsewhere for that matter—have been particularly successful in showing that questions about potential future pathways gain in urgency during this advanced stage of people's educational trajectories (Liechty 2003; Snellinger 2018; see also Jeffrey 2010b; Lukose 2010; Mains 2012). University students are often confronted with the immediate prospect of approaching an important milestone in their lives, namely, the completion of formal education. While these contributions provide a good starting point for my research into the future strategies of a newly educated generation in Nepal, they remain largely focused on young men belonging to upper-status groups. As such, they risk downplaying the extent to which young people internalize and act upon socially instilled future ideals differently depending on their social identities and their lived experiences.

With this in mind, I argue that the perspectives of the students of Patan Multiple Campus (hereafter Patan Campus) offer a particularly interesting vantage point from which to examine the various ways in which young people engage with and rework dominant representations of youth and related aspirations for the future. The 21 women and 19 men whose stories I recall in this book were between 21 and 36 years old and came from different socio-economic backgrounds. About half of the research participants had grown up within the urban Kathmandu Valley. The others had moved to the capital city more recently and originally came from other regions of Nepal, including some rural areas in the mountainous parts of eastern and western Nepal and in the hill region (full-fledged mountains by European standards of up to 3,000 metres altitude). However, all 40 research participants had in common that they were enrolled for a master's programme on Patan Campus in 2011–12.

At the time of my field research, Patan Campus was one of the 60 constituent campuses of Tribhuvan University (TU), Nepal's oldest and only state-run university. I reached the decision to base my research project on Patan Campus after giving thorough consideration to various criteria, including the composition of the student body, location, and accessibility. In comparison to private institutions of higher education, such as Kathmandu University, which is also situated within the Kathmandu Valley, Tribhuvan University served a much larger and more diverse student body. During the academic year 2011–12, a total of 389,460 students were enrolled at TU's central campus, its 60 constituent campuses, and its 826 affiliated colleges.[1]

Patan Campus was founded in 1954 at a time when efforts were intensified to establish a national system of higher education in Nepal. Most of the older colleges were initially set up not by the state but by private actors or through community-based initiatives. The resources necessary for the establishment of these colleges were mobilized mainly by members of the urban upper castes who wanted their offsprings to attain academic credentials needed to qualify for high-status positions in the government administration. In the same vein, Patan Campus was established at the edge of the ancient city of Patan, particularly known for its rich cultural heritage and located only 3 km south of the old centre of Kathmandu. Overall, half of the 21 colleges that were operating in Nepal in 1959 were situated within the Kathmandu Valley (Ministry of Education [MoE] 1970: 30–1). The establishment of a national system of higher education in the 1950s, therefore, manifested the socio–economic divide between the Kathmandu Valley and the rest of the country.

In the 1970s, all community-owned or privately managed colleges, including Patan Campus, were turned into constituent campuses of Tribhuvan University and placed under the administrative control of a national education committee appointed by the king (Lal 2000). The centralization of the provision of higher education ousted private investments in the higher education sector, with the result that the university and its constituent campuses had to rely entirely on

---

[1] For the enrolment figures and number of colleges, I referred to the statistics published on the web page of the university during the academic year 2011–12; see http://tribhuvan-university.edu.np/about-us/, accessed 25 July 2012.

the treasury. At the time of my field research, the national government still financed up to 90 per cent of the budget for TU's central departments and its constituent campuses. In contrast, affiliated colleges, that is, private or community-run institutions established from the 1980s onwards, did not receive any state-financed subsidies and maintained their own cost structure, including remunerations and tuition fees. While chronic underfunding and political disputes resulted in a deterioration of educational quality at TU campuses, many young Nepalis still benefited from state-financed higher education as a university education would otherwise be unaffordable for them.

I quickly came to understand that students' choices of where to study were primarily influenced by their financial capacity, the range of subjects offered by the institution, and the class schedule (Kölbel 2013). In order to reach out to young people from different social and geographical backgrounds, I therefore decided against the smaller private colleges, many of which only taught one or two programmes at intermediate (grades 11 and 12) and bachelor's level. Patan Campus, by contrast, offered both bachelor and master programmes in the fields of humanities, social sciences, management, and sciences. At the same time, the campus had a convenient size in terms of both its physical premises and the number of students enrolled (see Figure 2.1). It was small enough to ensure that I could introduce myself to the student community within a relatively short time, but it was also big enough to allow for the anonymity of the individual students participating in my research project.

The campus was located at the edge of the old centre of Patan, in close proximity to Pulchowk Engineering Campus, founded in 1972 as part of TU's Institute of Engineering, and Rato Bangala School, a privately run international school founded in 1992. Apart from the location, Patan Campus had little in common with these two other educational institutions, which were known for their highly selective admission procedures and comparatively high tuition fees. At Patan Campus, in contrast, any prospective student who had passed the qualifying lower degree and was able to pay the registration fee of Rs 150 was admitted for the courses taught at the departments of social sciences, humanities, and management throughout the academic year. Many students had decided to enrol at Patan Campus

Figure 2.1 View across the Kathmandu Valley with Patan Campus in the Foreground, January 2012
Source: Author

precisely because the lax regulations concerning admission and atten-dance allowed them to combine their university studies with other competing priorities, such as a full-time job or family commitments (see also Kölbel 2013, 2016).

Any study conducted on and around a university campus in Nepal needs to be cognizant of how student politics may come into play. The connection between higher education and national politics is deeply rooted in Nepal's history. Instances of student politics can be traced back to protests by university students against the rule of Ranas in 1947 (Hoftun, Raeper, and Whelpton 1999; Snellinger 2005). Subsequently, several students involved in these protests went into exile in India, where they first established the Nepali Congress, and later, the Communist Party of Nepal. The political heritage of these two parties continues to be of importance, with the national parties which claim to be descended from them having won the elections to the second Constituent Assembly held in November

2013 and the legislative elections held in 2017. Under the rule of the 'party-less' Panchayat regime (1960–90), student organizations further gained relevance in national politics as they were able to continue to operate as legal entities, while political parties were forced to go underground (Snellinger 2005). Since that time, most student leaders do not necessarily only fight for matters of direct concern to the university students they are supposed to represent, but also incorporate the political programmes of the national parties they are affiliated with (Snellinger 2005).

Initially, the involvement of young people in national politics was centred around Kathmandu's university campuses. This, however, changed with the emergence of the Maoist movement in the more rural and remote parts of Nepal during the latter half of the 1990s. This new political force quickly gained in popularity among rural youth, mainly because young people in rural Nepal severely lacked opportunities to attain a good education and to achieve a livelihood (Ghimire 2005; Pettigrew 2007; Pherali 2011; Zharkevich 2009). During the civil war between 1996 and 2006, many young people saw the underground existence of the Maoists as an opportunity to hold out against persisting inequalities (Mikesell 2006; Pherali 2011) and to broaden their outlook by personally experiencing life outside the confines of the village community (Pettigrew 2007; Zharkevich 2009). Since the end of the civil war in 2006, the Unified Communist Party of Nepal (Maoist) has been represented on the country's university campuses by its affiliated student activists just like any other national party. In this sense, all of the political student organizations based at university campuses in Nepal are essentially sister organizations of national parties, even to the extent that elections to the student unions are now taken as a proxy for country-wide elections to the national government (Snellinger 2007, 2018). In the light of these historical developments and continuing debates, most Nepalis have come to think of public university campuses, including Patan Campus, as microcosms of national party rivalries.

Patan, the third largest city in Nepal, was called by many locals by its original Sanskrit name, Lalitpur, or by its Newari name, Yala. Together with Kathmandu, Kirtipur, Madhyapur Thimi, and Bhaktapur, Patan was home to approximately 5 million people residing within the Kathmandu Valley. Even though the city of Patan officially maintained its independence from Kathmandu, most people, including the students of Patan Campus, considered Patan to be a kind of suburb, separated from the capital city only by the Bagmati River. Accordingly, my research setting did not remain confined to the site of the campus. Once I started visiting the campus regularly to meet with the students, my research site began to expand rapidly beyond the boundary of the wall that ran along the periphery of the campus premises. As I sought to adapt to the students' schedules, I ended up criss-crossing through the urban space with them on a daily basis. As the research participants lived and worked in different parts of the valley, I could never be sure how far away from the campus my efforts to conduct interviews with them and follow their daily routines would take me by the end of the day. As I was moving through the culturally multifaceted and highly dense but also discontinuous space of the urban Kathmandu Valley, I often found it difficult to locate 'the field' (cf. Clifford 1997) and decide when I was entering and exiting it. In this book, I therefore do not speak only specifically of the university students of Patan Campus but, more generally, of educated young people living, studying, and working in urban Nepal.

The Social Significance of Spatial Mobility

Estimates suggest that in recent years, between 500 and 1,500 Nepalis per day have left from the international airport in Kathmandu (Adhikari 2012; Deshar 2011). Many of these Nepalis are young people who go abroad in order to work in countries in the Gulf region or Southeast Asia (for example, Bruslé 2010; Graner and Gurung 2003), or to study at universities, mainly in North America, Europe, or Australia (for example, Sijapati and Hermann 2012; Valentin 2012a). In the USA, for example, Nepali students were the eleventh largest group of international students during the academic year 2010–11 and in Japan and Australia, they were the eighth largest (Institute of International Education [IIE] 2011). These figures indicate that even though Nepal is a relatively small and poor country, it is intimately tied up with large-scale developments happening across the globe.

This trend towards out-migration—described by some scholars as 'the Nepali exodus' (Sharma 2010)—has generated considerable debate within the Nepali society. On the one hand, international migration promises to be a way for young Nepalis to build a better future life for themselves and their families. Apart from contributing financial remittances, it is hoped that young migrants will also contribute to the country's development upon return by drawing from the knowledge and skills they have acquired abroad (Ghimire and Maharjan 2015). Critics, on the other hand, have warned against the heavy costs of this 'brain drain' and the great loss of youthful potential as Nepal's youth is seen to be primarily contributing to the wealth of other countries (Khare and Slany 2011).

As the debates continue to revolve primarily around young people's motivations behind foreign migration and the experiences of young migrants, little is known about how the increased mobility of some young people affects their peers at home. Yet, more than 90 per cent of Nepalis who enrol for higher education study at a university campus in their home country. Although they constitute the vast majority of the country's educated youth, these students have so far been much less visible in public and scholarly debates than those Nepali students who study abroad. However, I hold that spatial mobility plays a similarly important role in the lives of these young people—partly because images of and discourses about international student mobility have become an integral part of young people's everyday lives and partly because spatial mobility historically carries much significance for a person's social standing and the workings of society.

In the case of Nepali society, the relationship between spatial mobility and immobility is perhaps best explained with reference to the two local concepts of 'home' (*ghar*) and 'beyond' (*para*). Many people in Nepal identify with their 'home' not only because it is the land of the ancestors and often, though not always, their place of birth but also because it is a place of emotional and spiritual attachment. Drawing from field research conducted in Namsaling, a rural part of Ilam district located at the eastern border of Nepal, geographer Bhim P. Subedi (1999: 138) writes about people's relationship with the native home: '*Ghara*[2] is not just the house to live in and

---

[2] Subedi (1999) uses the more colloquial pronunciation of the term 'ghar' with an additional 'a'. Regardless of which spelling is preferred, the meaning of ghar and ghara is the same.

not something that can be anywhere and can be exchanged, but an irreplaceable centre of significance. It is neither limited to physical structure nor a physical space to carry on livelihood. It captures broader networks, intimate relations with the land and environment, and a place of rooted memory.'

In contrast, 'para' refers to any place beyond the regular boundaries of home. While para is not a preferred place to live for long, it is still deemed to be of great importance for people's life chances. By moving beyond the confines of the home community, a person is thought to acquire more knowledge and stand better chances of finding a job to earn a living. While ghar is the place to live (and to return to), para is the place to experience (Subedi 1999: 139). The insights that the individual obtains while away from home are seen to allow the wider community to keep pace with changing circumstances. Simultaneously, a profound sense of rootedness within the home community, which is usually demonstrated through regular visits, helps the individual to maintain a strong security network. Thus, the two concepts need to be understood as complementary and of significance for both those who move away and those who stay at home (Subedi 1999: 141).

Evidence suggests that Nepali people have been highly mobile between 'home' and 'beyond' for several centuries. In the eighteenth and nineteenth centuries, for example, people in Nepal moved from the hill region to the southern plains in search of better livelihood opportunities (Regmi 1978). Around the same time, Nepali men also started to migrate beyond the country's borders to Lahore (in today's Pakistan) to join the armed forces of the Sikh ruler, Ranjit Singh. This tradition is reflected in the name 'Lahures', which is still used today to refer to international labour migrants from Nepal (for example, Graner and Gurung 2003; Seddon, Adhikari, and Gurung 2001). Since 1816, Nepali men were systematically recruited into the (British) Indian Army (for example, Shrestha 1990). Others migrated to neighbouring India to work on the tea plantations in Darjeeling and Assam (Chettri 2013; Hoffman 2001). Estimates suggest that by the end of the nineteenth century, half of the population in Darjeeling was of Nepali origin (Caplan 1970; Shrestha 1990).

India has continued to be the primary destination of migrants from Nepal to date. This is partly because of the open border between the two countries, officially recognized in the 1950 Treaty of Peace and Friendship between India and Nepal, which allows citizens of the two nations to enter the neighbouring country without a passport or other immigration documents (Panday 1999). In contrast, foreign migration from Nepal to destinations other than India had long been restricted by national policies. In the course of state decentralization in the 1990s and 2000s, however, it became easier for Nepali people to obtain travel documents (Graner 2010). In addition, the Nepali government has been actively promoting foreign labour migration to countries in Southeast Asia and the Gulf region since the end of the twentieth century.

Legal restrictions, nonetheless, continue to apply to female migration. In 1998, the government introduced a new law that prohibited women under the age of 30 from travelling to the Gulf region. The regulation was imposed in response to repeated cases of gender-based violence against female migrants working in Arab countries (Thieme and Wyss 2005: 63–4). The ban was partly lifted in 2003, but was reinforced in 2012, after it was made public that several Nepali women working as domestic servants in Gulf countries had, once again, become victims of sexual and psychological exploitation. These official regulations notwithstanding, the number of female labour migrants has been consistently on the rise. Many of these women rely on unlicensed recruitment agents, who channel them abroad via the open border with India. Such informal migration routes, however, expose female migrants to even greater risks (for example, Adhikari 2012; Gurung 2003). Even so, the large majority of foreign migrants from Nepal are still likely to be male. Official statistics available for the years 2006–12, for example, show that over 90 per cent of the 1.7 million people who left Nepal during this period to work in countries other than India were men (Adhikari 2012: 20).

In view of these population movements, it becomes apparent that Nepalis have long been moving to other places, both within and beyond the nation's borders, in search of better livelihood opportunities. Considering that only 15 per cent of Nepal's total area of 147,181 sq. km is arable (CBS 2013), the basic need to grow food has been an important driving force behind population movements from the hills and mountains in the north of Nepal to the fertile lands in the southern plains. A new wave of internal migration was also triggered by the emergence of manufacturing industries in the Kathmandu Valley in the late 1980s and the 1990s. The workers employed in these labour-intensive industries, for the most part, were women and adolescents from the rural areas in the central and eastern regions of Nepal (Graner 2001: 256–7). Many of them had not completed basic levels of formal education (Graner 2001). Even though the conditions for unskilled and semi-skilled labourers have significantly deteriorated in the urban labour market since the mid-1990s, people have continued to migrate to the capital city from other parts of Nepal. As a result, the Kathmandu Valley has emerged as one of the fastest-growing urban agglomerations in South Asia (Muzzini and Aparicio 2013).

With the downturn in export-oriented industries in the early 1990s, foreign-currency earnings initially declined rapidly. In response, the Nepali government, in cooperation with foreign employment agencies (colloquially known as 'manpower agencies'), significantly stepped up efforts to promote labour migration beyond national borders to emerging economies in Southeast Asia and the Gulf region. As a result, in the past two decades, foreign remittances have increased significantly. According to official records, in 2011, remittance income amounted to almost Rs 300 million, that is, 22 per cent of gross domestic product (Adhikari 2012: 24). This figure is the highest in South Asia and the fifth highest in the world (see also Khare and Slany 2011). Nevertheless, some scholars have argued that these official statistics still grossly underestimate the total volume of remittances received by Nepali households, suggesting that it is more likely to be between Rs 20 billion and Rs 60 billion (for a discussion of these figures, see Graner 2010: 28).

There is more agreement regarding the profile of foreign workers from Nepal: the large majority of them are men aged 20–30 years, who often have dropped out of secondary school (for example, Adhikari 2012; Bruslé 2010; Graner 2010). The money these young men send home is primarily spent to cover more immediate domestic expenditures as opposed to long-term investments. Even so, foreign remittances have saved many families, specifically in rural areas of Nepal, from falling below the poverty line. As Elvira Graner (2001, 2010) has argued, these developments have major implications for the village economy. Whereas recruitment into the carpet factories in Kathmandu is essentially done via family and village networks, access to the international labour market is almost exclusively controlled by foreign employment agencies. These middlemen charge about Rs 60,000–Rs 90,000—an amount for which most Nepali labourers need to work at least for 2–3 years (Graner 2010: 37). Consequently, informal credit systems have seen a tremendous revival in rural communities. In addition, it is questionable whether rural households in Nepal can still be classified as 'agricultural', considering that foreign remittances constitute a major source of income for many of these families. In view of these most recent economic developments, experts have emphasized that Nepal has started to shift from being a predominately agrarian economy to one increasingly dependent on remittances (Seddon, Adhikari, and Gurung 2002; Sharma 2012).

Furthermore, there exist a number of non-economic factors that have contributed to high levels of spatial mobility within the Nepali society. For one, both internal and international migration accelerated significantly due to political instabilities. It is assumed that up to 600,000 people were displaced over the 10-year period of the civil war between the government forces and the Maoists (for example, Aditya, Upreti, and Adhikary 2006: 101; Ghimire 2010: 91). More recently, in 2007, an additional 6,000–8,000 people were forced to leave their homes in the Terai, the southern plains of Nepal, as political protests demanding the formation of a Madhes autonomous region escalated into a violent conflict between the different communities residing in the southern parts of Nepal (Arnøy 2012; Poudel and Ghimire 2010). More than half of the Nepali people displaced in these two conflicts are thought to have left the country. However, the overwhelming majority of those who stayed in Nepal fled to the capital city and other urban centres, which, in addition to safety, were seen to offer a whole range of better living conditions, including educational facilities, health services, and income opportunities. Even though the life of internally displaced persons (IDPs) continues to be fraught with difficulties, most of them, and especially the younger ones, have often been able to benefit in some way from the opportunities available in the urban centres (for example, Carney and Madsen 2009; Ghimire 2010; Nelson 2013). Consequently, most IDPs—whether rich or poor—would prefer to stay permanently, despite the fact that the government continues to promote a definite return to the place of origin as the only (and least expensive) solution for the predicament of the IDPs in Nepal (Ghimire 2010).

People's decision to leave their natal homes also needs to be understood within the context of social norms. A very common reason behind rural-to-rural migration in Nepal is marriage. In Nepali Hindu tradition, it is common for the bride to join the groom's family after the marriage and to continue to stay with her in-laws even if the husband passes away (Subedi 1999: 128). In this sense, female migration is not a new social phenomenon in Nepal but has, for long, been an integral part of the lives of most Nepali women. In a similar manner, some research suggests that migration also constitutes a kind of rite of passage to adulthood in the male life cycle. Studies conducted in villages in the western hills of Nepal describe the tradition of 'escape' (*bhāgne*), in which teenage boys leave their home communities without consulting their parents and go to the city or to India (Sharma 2009: 312–13; Thieme and Wyss 2005: 73). Often, they only return back home after having earned some money. In this way, young men can demonstrate that they are adult enough to provide for their families and, hence, can gain full acceptance into the adult community. These practices suggest that migration has long been institutionalized in the culture of various communities in Nepal.

During the second half of the twentieth century, however, there were some changes in the ways in which Nepalis thought about migration, its purposes, and potential destinations. At that time, the primacy of Kathmandu as the economic and political centre of the country was further reinforced through development discourses and pedagogic strategies. In the textbooks used in schools across the country, the city was depicted as a place of 'progress', 'development', 'modernisation' (Pigg 1992: 495) and an urban childhood as 'diligent study' and 'carefree play' (Pigg 1992: 501). The village, in contrast, was associated with underdevelopment and backwardness, and a rural childhood with poor living conditions and hard work (Pigg 1992; see also Gellner 2004; Lind Petersen 2011). At the university level, the government, through Tribhuvan University, implemented the National Development Service (NDS), a civic service programme which made it mandatory for students studying at master's level in

Kathmandu during the 1970s to spend one year working in rural areas of the country, usually as teachers in public schools that had been newly established in various villages (Messerschmidt, Yadama, and Silwal 2007; Shakya 2008). The aim of these educational policies was to bridge the divide between the rural and urban areas and to integrate developmental discourses into the formal training of the younger generation. However, the approach taken essentially implied a strong dichotomy, with the developed city on the one hand, and the underdeveloped rest of the country on the other. Even at present, many Nepalis still seem to believe that 'development' and 'progress' is not something generated locally, at the village level, but something concentrated in and emanating from the capital city.

In the 1990s and 2000s, modern technologies, such as the radio, television, mobile phones, and, more recently, the Internet, became an integral part of daily life in Kathmandu and opened up new ways for Nepali people to connect on an international scale. The information circulated by the global media have fuelled desires to take advantage of better educational and occupational opportunities abroad and to escape the difficulties of daily life in Nepal (Adhikari 2010; Liechty 2010: xi). Fantasies of earning enough money and gaining social prestige, however, are constantly belied by stories of migrants and returnees about the difficult and sometimes horrific living conditions abroad (Kunreuther 2006). Such ambiguities notwithstanding, the 'outside world' often seems to be within closer reach for many young people in Kathmandu than any village in Nepal. Stacy Pigg (1992: 493) even suggests that 'the most elite, educated, and urbanised, are so socially distant from village life in Nepal that for them to go to a village is tantamount to visiting an alien land.' In this sense, public debates about global migration trends have further reinforced Kathmandu's locality as the country's 'gateway and gatekeeper' to the outside world (see also Liechty 2003: 40).

Since the beginning of the twenty-first century, the number of young Nepalis who go abroad on a student visa has increased rapidly. Previously, only very few Nepalis whose families belonged to the established elites in Kathmandu went abroad to attend educational institutions outside Nepal (Kölbel 2017). Liechty (2003: 215) emphasizes this point in his ethnographic study, noting that 'while the elite construct their dreams around imagined lives in distant global culture/power centres, for the middle class, perceptions of the future are still very much centred on Kathmandu.' Over the past two decades, however, Kathmandu's new middle class has also increasingly made it a priority for their children to attain an international education. In some cases, immediate security concerns and far-reaching uncertainties about the country's economic and political future have made many middle-class families send their children abroad (see also Valentin 2012b). At the same time, processes of internationalization in the higher education sector have opened up new and somewhat more affordable opportunities of attaining a foreign degree. In particular, European countries, Australia, Hong Kong, and Singapore have launched a number of educational initiatives and new immigration regulations with the aim to become more established in the global education market (for example, Baas 2007; Brooks and Waters 2011; Valentin 2012a). In this way, images of and discourses about international student mobility have become an integral part of young Nepalis' everyday lives, with the result that even those young people who have never travelled abroad now construct their biographies with reference to dominant imaginaries attached to foreign migration.

Bringing 'Ordinary' Youth Back into the Conversation

A review of dominant representations of the educated youth in urban Nepal reveals that the concept of youth agency tends to be bound up with notions of resourcefulness, ingenuity, resistance, and change—whether for better or worse. In this chapter, I have outlined a number of large-scale political agitations, economic transitions, and social transformations witnessed by Nepali society since the 1980s. This turbulent period in the country's history saw the end of Hindu monarchy and the proclamation of a secular republic in 2008, a growing dependency of the country's economy on foreign remittances, and the establishment of a mass education system. The public discourses accompanying these transformations promoted and manifested a specific sociocultural construct of the 'educated youth', one which depicted the newly educated younger generation as society's hope for a more prosperous future.

Similar conceptions of youth feature prominently in a range of policies, programmes, and discourses about youth activism and youth participation across the globe (for example, Durham 2008; Flanagan and Faison 2001; Højlund et al. 2011). In order to move beyond such a narrow understanding of the concept of youth agency, it is necessary to address underlying methodological issues. Even though it is generally recognized that the category of 'youth' does not constitute a homogeneous group of people, the analysis presented in this chapter reveals that particular conceptions that associate youth primarily with notions of rupture and deviance continue to be at work. I have shown that these images of youth are consistently reproduced through dominant discourses about the role of young people in wider society, mainly because they remain largely focused on highly visible forms of youth activism. In Nepal, much of the relevant debate either praises the potential of the country's newly educated younger generation to find solutions for a range of problems faced by the wider society or warns against the sometimes destructive force of youth agency. The kind of actions that are selected for attention, including student politics and foreign migration, further reinforce the idea that young people's collective actions constitute a clear break from the existing social system.

Such universalizing and often simplified representations of youth, however, tend to ignore that educated young people have to negotiate a whole range of social pressures and structuring forces and that they do so in various and uneven ways. As a result, some young people may not identify themselves with these dominant depictions and, consequently, may not think of these public discourses as a source of inspiration. Based on an analysis of high-profile policy statements of international organizations advocating children's rights, Kraftl (2008: 83) explicitly notes that 'despite the best intentions of policymakers and charities ..., simple representations of childhood-hope that reinforce a stereotype of young people ... *may* succeed in obscuring any sense of hope (and even agency) in the present or near-future.' In this book, I therefore examine how young people in Nepal, and specifically public university students in Kathmandu, were tied up in and related to such public rhetoric. Rather than asking solely what youth agency means to others—be it scholars or policymakers, the media or wider society—I hold that it is important to ask what youth agency means to young people themselves. I propose that, by taking up this question, it becomes possible to move beyond prevalent depictions of youth towards a more refined understanding of the role of youth in processes of social change.

For this purpose, I want to bring 'ordinary' youth back into the conversation. The students I worked with have so far remained largely invisible in both public and scholarly debates. They have not had any first-hand experiences of travelling abroad and also, like the vast majority of university students in Nepal, have sought to maintain a neutral stance towards party politics. At the same time, they belong to a generation of young Nepalis whose lives have been forcefully shaped by large-scale social, economic, and political changes. In this respect, it is vital to remain attentive to the ways in which established markers of social difference—be it gender, caste/ethnicity, class, or geographical origin—continue to shape young people's educational and occupational experiences and, in relation to this, their future orientations. While previous studies of young people studying at universities in Nepal generally provide a good starting point to look into these issues, they have primarily focused on young people belonging to upper-status groups and especially young men (Liechty 2003; Snellinger 2010). In contrast, I sought to engage with both male and female students of different caste/ethnic and geographical origin. By including young people belonging to social groups that have previously not been represented at university level and, hence, continue to be less visible among the student community, I suggest that it becomes possible to shed new light on the concept of youth agency, specifically on the ways in which young people's capacity to act links to their social and spatial identities. To this end, my research into the future strategies of the students of Patan Campus ties in with the ongoing efforts to broaden the scope of youth research in order to develop a more comprehensive understanding of the concept of agency.

Rather than solely reviewing the historical and cultural factors which serve as the backdrop for young people's experiences and perceptions, I have begun locating the concept of youth within the discourses and agendas of a range of different actors in Nepal. In the political agendas, school materials, and development programmes, the category of youth has been commonly depicted in a rather dualistic manner. On the one hand, youth is seen to be a source of hope for a better future as the younger generation seems to be uniquely poised to take advantage of a whole range of new opportunities. On the other, youth is directly associated with heightened levels of uncertainty and anxiety as young Nepalis no longer follow familiar life trajectories and, thus, seem to increasingly depart from established practices and beliefs. The empirical chapters that follow continue the theme of young people's life chances and the future visions ascribed to the practices of educated youth, by focusing on the future aspirations and the lived experiences of a group of young Nepalis who, in 2011–12, were all studying, working, and living in Kathmandu.

3

Fashioning the Future
Students' Spatial and Social (Im)Mobilities

One day in early March 2012, I was walking with Shreya, a 25-year-old Chhetri woman, through the narrow roads of a residential area to the east of Kathmandu's old city centre. Shreya and I had met in the morning on Patan Campus, where she was enrolled as a master's student in the economics department, and we had decided to continue our conversation on her way to work. Holi, the festival of water and colours, was coming up and so I was in a constant state of alert, knowing that it was part of the celebrations that kids threw water balloons on passers-by from the roof terraces of the residential houses. However, Shreya assured me that we were safe: 'We are not like schoolgirls or even students doing their bachelor's degrees. They get teased by the boys and all they can do is to look down. But we know how to defend ourselves, so the guys just leave us alone. That's why education is so important for us women.' While I was somewhat distracted by two young boys who stood sniggering on the terrace of the house we were walking past at that moment, I asked in return: 'So, they only target young girls and not adults with their water bombs?' Shreya laughed: 'We are also young! But education has made us more confident. For example, speaking like this. See, even after I passed School Leaving Certificate (SLC) [tenth grade],

I was not able to speak like this. But now, I can easily chat along and talk to other people. This is because of education.' According to Shreya, it was possible to distinguish an 'uneducated', timid young woman from an 'educated', confident young woman based on small gestures, such as looking up when walking past a group of men or feeling at ease when talking to other people.

Born in the mid-1980s, Shreya and the other students I met on Patan Campus belonged to a generation of Nepalis who had benefited from a so-far unprecedented expansion of the formal education sector in Nepal. The provision of higher education in Nepal dates back to 1918, when Tri-Chandra College was founded to educate the country's political elite (Whelpton 2005: 83). Even though efforts were intensified to introduce a Western-style education system countrywide in the 1950s, opportunities to attain a formal, let alone an academic, education remained highly restricted for most of the second half of twentieth century. A survey of 804 university graduates who obtained their degrees between 1974 and 1981 in Nepal shows that half of them were from the Kathmandu Valley and 85 per cent of them belonged to the upper castes, namely, Brahmin, Chhetri, and Newar (Kayastha 1985: 25–40). The study also reveals that less than one-fifth of the graduates were women (Kayastha 1985: 26).

Enrolment numbers only started to increase significantly in the 1980s and 1990s, when a new middle class emerged in Kathmandu. An academic education was considered to be key for the production and reproduction of socio-economic privileges and became a kind of 'ideology' of the propertied classes (Liechty 2003; Sijapati 2005). The magnitude of this increased demand for higher education is rendered visible in the profileration of colleges and universities, especially within the Kathmandu Valley. In 1980, the state-run Tribhuvan University, which was then the country's only university, began to provide affiliations to a number of private and community colleges in order to respond to the heightened admission pressure. Within the first 15 years, 140 affiliated colleges were established (TU 1996). Another 15 years later, in 2011–12, the number of affiliated colleges had increased exponentially, reaching 826 in total (TU 2012). Within the same time frame, three new universities were founded: a private one in the Kathmandu Valley and two community-funded universities in urban centres outside the valley. This rapid expansion of the tertiary education sector has significantly shaped the life paths of the young people featuring in this study.

Most of the students I spoke with were convinced that the opportunity to continue to higher levels of education had been a turning point in their lives. Chitra, for example, proudly told me that she was the first woman of the Tamang community in her village to obtain a master's degree. She grew up as the oldest of four siblings in a rural part of Parsa district, close to Nepal's border with India, and had moved to the capital city together with her cousin in 2009. At the time of my fieldwork, Chitra had already passed all her exams and was busy writing up her master's thesis. She was excited about the prospect of graduating in the near future and told me:

> My parents did not believe that I would ever reach this level of education. Now, they are very proud. I feel like I have become somebody. I have made my own identity. My father's name is Ram Bir. But I am not Ram Bir's daughter. Ram Bir is Chitra Maya's father. That is not only how I feel but also how people at home think of me now that I have moved to Kathmandu and studied at university.

When Chitra told me more about her educational trajectory, I started to understand why she attached such great significance and pride to her educational achievements. She had been forced to drop out of primary school at the age of seven due to the poor economic situation of her family, and was only able to return to school when she was 15 years old. At that time, she was admitted in fifth grade. She remembered how embarrassing it was for her initially, since she was far behind her classmates who were half her age: 'I just knew the ABC. I did not know plus or minus. Imagine, such kind of person being admitted to grade 5!' She, however, caught up quickly and was allowed to skip one year and continue with seventh grade the following school year. In her final year at school, her parents wanted her to discontinue despite the fact that she was the second best in her class. 'I don't blame my parents. Back then, I was also unable to think of any future plans beside marriage.' Her teachers convinced her parents to allow Chitra to take the final exams for the SLC at the end of tenth grade. She passed, much to her surprise. With the support of her cousin, who encouraged her to continue her studies—first at a college in Birganj, the district's headquarters, and subsequently at Patan

Campus—Chitra had managed to decline her parents' attempts to arrange for her marriage numerous times and, instead, had started to make her own plans for the future: 'I can still get married later in my life. Now, I have big dreams. I am working to save up money for my PhD.'

A macro perspective of Nepal's tertiary education sector implies that Chitra was an exemption to the rule. Student enrolment data that I obtained on Patan Campus at the beginning of the academic year 2011–12 revealed that historical disparities with regard to students' gender, caste/ethnic identities, and geographical origins remain largely intact (Kölbel 2015). Two-thirds of the students of Patan Campus were men. More than two-thirds of the students (both male and female) belonged to upper castes, namely, Brahmin and Chhetri, who only represent about one-third of Nepal's total population. Equally over-represented were Newars, the ethnic/linguistic group that has long dominated the social and cultural life within the Kathmandu Valley. Other ethnic/linguistic groups, formerly known as 'tribes' and now commonly called Janajatis,[1] together constitute one-third of the country's population. On Patan Campus, however, less than 12 per cent of the students belonged to one of these ethnic groups. Similarly under-represented were Madhesis, that is, Nepalis of Indian, Hindu origin who reside in the Terai, the southern plains of Nepal. People, who are now collectively referred to as Dalits and who were previously considered to be 'untouchable' under the Hindu caste system, make up for 13 per cent of the country's population. Constituting a mere 2 per cent of the student body, Dalits were hardly represented at all among the students of Patan Campus. With regard to the nature and extent of unequal representation of different social groups, Patan Campus was no different than any other public university campus in Nepal (see specifically Bhatta et al. 2008). In the 2010s, a university education still appeared to be a privilege of upper-status groups, and especially of young men.

---

[1] In most sociological surveys in Nepal, Newars are listed separately from the collective category of the Janajatis, despite being officially recognized as an ethnic group. This is a sensible distinction to make because Newars, and especially those residing in the Kathmandu Valley, are generally in a better socio-economic position than most other ethnic groups.

Yet, I found that these figures hide a number of trends which suggest that patterns of social inequality have started to change or, at least, have become more equivocal. A closer look at the statistical data revealed that in most of the social sciences courses, gender parity had been reached. In addition, about two-thirds of the students of Patan Campus grew up in other parts of the country: 60 of the 75 districts of Nepal were listed by them as places of origin. Many of them belonged to ethnic groups or lower castes and, often, were the first in their extended families to continue to higher education. Furthermore, the apparent under-representation of Madhesis concealed that many young Nepalis living along the open border with India were studying at universities and colleges in India.

More importantly perhaps, social differences—be it in terms of people's gender, caste, or class backgrounds—seemed to be of little importance for the ways in which students interacted with one another while on campus. According to Dipendra, a young Dalit born in 1984, he socialized with his fellow students on campus in an entirely different manner than he used to be able to during his schooldays:

> I was not allowed into someone else's house. Also, in school at lunch-time, I was always the last who got his plate of food and some boys would refuse to sit next to me. The caste system is deeply rooted in people's minds and it takes a long time to change. If I would not have continued my education, the situation would probably still be the same. But education has a big impact on the way we think and interact with others. I don't see any discriminating attitudes among students on campus.

I often joined Dipendra and his friends by the tea stalls to warm up with hot milk tea or share a small snack. One time, we talked about our preferences for tea. Dipendra had never tried the salty tea, which one of his classmates, an upper-caste Hindu girl, had ordered. The girl freely offered Dipendra to take a sip from her glass before she drank the remaining tea herself. I had been told often enough that my lips should not touch a bottle or a glass when I drank from it because water is believed to be a transmitter of impurity in Hindu tradition. It was, therefore, remarkable that such kind of gestures, like drinking from the same glass, were part of students' everyday

interactions on campus, whereas it would not have been at all acceptable for them to do so in most other contexts of their daily lives in
Kathmandu.

***

Patan Campus had a large catchment area. Only four out of the 40
students I got to know better over the course of my fieldwork lived
within walking distance of the campus. Most of their peers, however,
easily took an hour or two depending on traffic to commute from
home to campus. On a Sunday in December 2011, I was invited
by Namita, a 26-year-old lower-caste Newar woman, to her family's home. The neighbourhood where Namita grew up and still lived
with her parents and her two siblings was located on the outskirts in
the south of the city, approximately 15 km from campus. We met
at the campus gate at 9:30 a.m. after classes had finished. Namita
asked me whether I preferred to take a tuk-tuk (a three-wheeled,
propane-powered taxi) to the main road. She normally walked to
save money and so, we walked. We walked at a good pace but constantly had to slow down to avoid honking motorbikes, porters with
their heavy loads, piles of rubbish by the roadside, and stray dogs.
After 20 minutes, we reached the main road from where we took
the bus south along the Ring Road. We changed at Satdobato into a
super-crowded microbus (12-seater Toyota minivan). Namita and I
stood inside squeezed behind the sliding door, while the busboy and
two other passengers were hanging outside the open sliding door. We
had to get off at each stop to let other passengers out. After four or
five stops, we managed to get a seat. The traffic was less thick now,
which meant that the driver started speeding along an increasingly
bumpy road. We had to change once more into another microbus.
Every time we changed, Namita showed her student ID, even though
nobody asked for it. By the time we reached the final stop, it was
11:30 a.m. Walking for another 15 minutes past some fields and
newly built three-storeyed houses, we finally reached Namita's home.
On the way back, I was again stuck in traffic for 2 hours. By the time
I reached home that night, I only wrote a short note in my research
diary, saying: 'I am totally exhausted. No idea how Namita manages
to make this trip on a daily basis.'

I asked Namita about her commute the next day, when I met her and her three best friends on campus. All of them agreed that the daily commute between their homes, the campus, and their workplaces was time-consuming, exhausting, and costly—especially during the cold season, when prices increased every other week due to shortages of petrol and gas. Although their student ID cards entitled them to a 47 per cent discount, fares for public transport significantly cut their budgets. Namita calculated that she paid Rs 79.5 for the daily commute, which was Rs 12 more than a year ago when she had enrolled for the master's programme in sociology on Patan Campus. The same amount of money would have paid for a full meal in one of the eateries close to the campus premises. However, double-digit inflation rates had driven up prices not only for transportation but also for accommodation and food items in the capital city.

Namita's line of reasoning was immediately taken up by her friend Deepa, a 25-year-old Brahmin woman who had moved to Kathmandu from a small town in Morang district four years previously. In Deepa's opinion, constant price increases made it particularly difficult for people living in other parts of Nepal to gain an accurate idea of the cost of living in the Kathmandu Valley. She had also grossly underestimated the extent to which even basic living expenses would quickly deplete the financial resources available to her when she had moved to Kathmandu. During the first five months in Kathmandu, she had to live on a meagre budget of Rs 1,500: 'I was sharing a small room, which was both kitchen and bedroom, with my cousin and two other people. We were living under such poor conditions. Kathmandu had been an unknown place for me and I just thought, "Oh, where am I lost!"' The group of friends calculated that their basic expenses easily added up to Rs 7,000 per month. If, however, the parental home was located outside the Kathmandu Valley and one had to rent a room, monthly expenses were closer to Rs 20,000.

Without their families' support, it would have been impossible for most of the students I met on the campus to study in university, let alone in Kathmandu. Out of the 40 students I interviewed, 32 explicitly mentioned that their parents financed their educational expenses either in part or in full. In comparison with other institutions of higher education in Kathmandu, Patan Campus charged rather low tuition fees that, in 2011–12, ranged from Rs 8,000 to Rs 45,000 per year depending on the specific course. However, considering that Nepal's average per capita income was reported to be Rs 46,000 per annum in 2011 (*The Kathmandu Post* 2011), even this amount stretched the budgets of most of my respondents' families. Even so, parents were sometimes willing to make substantial financial sacrifices to invest in their children's formal education.

For the parental generation, formal education had often been less accessible due to financial constraints, early marriage, or because secondary schools were non-existent in rural areas outside the Kathmandu Valley. Most of my respondents' parents had, therefore, been forced to discontinue their education at lower levels of schooling. On average, mothers had completed three years and fathers had completed nine years of schooling. Deepa's mother, for example, knew how to read and write in Nepali but had never been able to attain any formal schooling. Her father had acquired basic levels of schooling and used to earn a small but regular salary as a lower-level civil servant for the local electricity supplier until he retired in 2010. When I met Deepa in 2011, the father's pension continued to be the main source of income for the family of six. On the topic of the financial resources needed to study at university, Deepa explained:

> My father took out a loan to pay for our education—Rs 10 lakh [1 million]. By now my parents have sold parts of our land to pay back some of the money. But 5–6 lakh are still left. I respect them a lot for that; for giving us the opportunity to study in Kathmandu. At the moment, they still need to send us money. But when I earn a good income, I will send money back [pause]—after two or three years, maybe.

Her friend, Sadhika, who at the time of my fieldwork was 28 years old and had a husband and a 3-year-old daughter, shook her head in response and remarked: 'They sell their land to provide for their children's education. And after that if the child doesn't get a good job, what will they do? Their land is gone! Education also won't work! They will have to face many problems.' Sadhika articulated a concern shared by many of her peers, namely, that fixed assets, such as the family's property or lifetime savings, were used for investments into an uncertain future.

The link between an academic education and a salaried employment, however, had become manifested in the social consciousness. Ever since Tribhuvan University was founded in 1959, 'the production of skilled manpower essential for the country's development' had been listed in the university's mission statement as the first of its four main purposes and objectives (TU 1996, 2012). The first few batches of university graduates were indeed easily absorbed into the newly emerging economic sector for tertiary activities, and often occupied respectable posts in the government service or the formal education sector (TU 1996). Those who secured a job in the civil sector during the 1970s and the 1980s—most of whom were upper-caste educated men—could be relatively confident to be able to claim a space in Kathmandu's emerging middle class (Liechty 2003). From the perspectives of the parental generation, an academic education therefore held the promise of a successful career and a financially secure future (Liechty 2003; Valentin 2011).

Whilst students were committed to meet their parents' expectations and to support their families, they were greatly concerned about the extent to which their families' financial situation depended on their success at university and, later, within the job market. The large majority of students enrolled at Patan Campus, therefore, sought to work alongside their studies. Almost half of the students I interviewed, including Sadhika and Namita, were employed in the private education sector. In order to be hired as a private tutor or school-teacher, it was often sufficient to have passed the SLC. Accordingly, some of the students had accumulated a remarkable amount of work experience. Sadhika, for example, had been employed by an English-medium school already for seven years as a teacher of English and sociology at lower secondary school level and was paid Rs 8,000 per month. To supplement her income, Sadhika also gave private tutorials in the evening three times a week. With her husband also working as a private schoolteacher, they earned just about enough to cover their living expenses. However, Sadhika urgently wanted to change her profession and find a job that matched her interest and academic qualifications in the field of rural development. She explained to me: 'The problem with private schools is that the school itself is respected. The teacher is not! The owners, they are very rich. They have their own cars. They have a good house. That's why the school is respected. But the teachers are not.'

Despite the fact that teaching represents one of the tenets of Hinduism, the social status attached to the profession of a schoolteacher in Nepali society was surprisingly low. Students of natural sciences were particularly concerned about being trapped in the teaching profession. Nepali schoolchildren were taught from an early age that a degree in natural sciences is highly prestigious as it is generally perceived to be more difficult and also more expensive than courses in the fields of humanities or social sciences. Whether the course actually enhanced students' employability and equipped them with the skills needed in the local labour market often appeared to be less important than the social prestige attached to a certain subject. As a result, several respondents anxiously noted that the educational qualifications they had obtained did not facilitate their career development. One of the students from the physics department aptly summarized this point by saying: 'We are all *khetālā* here. Even doctors are *khetālā* in Nepal.' The term 'khetālā' actually refers to day labourers and specifically to those working in the fields—a low-pay, low-prestige job which is considered to be entirely inappropriate for an educated person. For exactly these reasons, however, the term appeared to provide an apposite analogy for the occupational status held by many young Nepalis I met on Patan Campus.

***

When I first told Ameena about my research into young people's lives in Kathmandu and their aspirations for the future, she did not see the need for any investigations or much explanation. In her opinion, the answer was easy enough: 'These days you study, you complete your +2 [grades 11 and 12] and you go abroad for your bachelor's degree and only there you also earn money. This has become a fashion for everybody, really.' When I first spoke with Ameena in October 2011, she was 25 years old and about to start the second year of her master's programme. Her description, therefore, did not match her own educational trajectory or that of any of the other students I met on Patan Campus. None of them had ever applied to a foreign university, let alone gone abroad at some stage of their educational careers. At the same time, Ameena rightly summed up that the completion of upper secondary school (in colloquial language commonly referred to as +2) and bachelor's level constitute natural cut-off points in Nepal's formal education system and that a growing number of young Nepalis decide to continue their education abroad at these points in their lives. Statistical records from the MoE in Kathmandu give an idea of the extent to which studying abroad had become a 'fashion': Between 2011 and 2015, the number of young Nepalis who left the country on a student visa tripled (Ghimire 2015).

In Kathmandu, this quest for an international education is evident in the vast number of international schools that have opened since the beginning of the twenty-first century. These mostly privately run schools pride themselves on imparting excellent English-language skills and are often accredited with conducting advanced international degree courses, mostly in the form of British A-Levels (cf. Hayden 2011; Lowe 2000). In addition, they usually provide extra guidance to their students in terms of career counselling and alumni support. Information that I obtained from two of these schools suggest that, at the time of my field research, an estimated 60–80 per cent of the schools' graduates continued their education abroad, primarily in the USA, Europe, or Australia. However, the price for this stepping stone abroad is high. An article published in a Nepali daily newspaper in 2009 indicates that the tuition fees charged by these schools over the course of a year easily amount to more than double of Nepal's average per capita income (Dhakal 2009). Leaving aside admission fees and other costs, the schools charge between Rs 5,555 and Rs 13,000 per month at the secondary level. The financial burden notwithstanding, middle-class families in Kathmandu increasingly seek out these international schools in the hope that they allow their children to make a smooth transition straight from school to a university abroad. From the perspective of Kathmandu's middle class, a foreign degree promises to be a way for the offsprings to distinguish themselves from the growing number of educated young Nepalis from less privileged backgrounds whose increased participation in higher education represents a potential threat to the established class hierarchy (Adhikari 2010; Kölbel 2018; Sijapati and Hermann 2012; Valentin 2015).

The large majority of the students enrolled at Patan Campus previously attended public schools which, they argued, put them at a disadvantage in some respects: 'If you go to a private school, you have the opportunity to study in English medium and to interact with people from quite well-off families. I've never been to a private education institution. I went to a government school and now I am again at a government campus. That's why my English is poor.' When judged based on specific input and output indicators, such as classroom facilities and students' command of English, private institutions, by and large, outperformed public schools (for example, Thapa 2013, 2015). While the former could avail themselves of a steady stream of income in the form of tuition fees, the latter were chronically underfunded. Most people I spoke with in Kathmandu, therefore, thought that the most expensive schools provided the best education (see also Caddell 2006).

The appeal to study abroad, however, still formed an integral part of the everyday lives of the young Nepalis who studied in Patan Campus. All of the students I spoke with seemed to know of somebody who was studying abroad. Tulasi, for example, was confident that he would follow his friends' example and move to a Western country: 'Either Denmark or Australia. In both countries, I have friends who study and work there. They told me that, in these countries, you are allowed to work and earn some money after completing your studies. They also have a physics background.' Tulasi, who, in 2011, was enrolled for the master's programme at the physics department in Patan Campus, was the oldest son of a Brahmin family and originally from Pathari, a semi-urban area in southeast Nepal. The more we talked about his friends in Denmark and Australia, the less confident Tulasi became. He did not know for how long his friends had been abroad, in which city they lived, which university they attended, and whether or not they had completed their studies. Eventually, Tulasi explained: 'I don't know. [pause] About their jobs and their studies, I don't know. I contacted them on Facebook. What they are doing there and at which level they are studying, I don't know. It has been a long time since we've been in contact.'

The Internet and more specifically, social networking sites, have been identified by several researchers working with international students as an important means for young people to gather information before they travel abroad (Collins 2012; Lee 2008) and also to expand their social networks beyond their immediate circle of family or friends (Beech 2015; Ellison et al. 2007). Yet, I found that young people's ability to obtain reliable information about studying abroad from social networking sites depends significantly on how exactly they are placed within these networks (for more information, see Kölbel 2018). In the conversations I had with students in Kathmandu about their peers abroad, it became apparent that most of them spoke of a distant relative, a former colleague, or a friends' friend with whom they had barely been in contact before. These people moved abroad to study. The photographs and anecdotes shared through online networking sites often revolved around their peers' leisure activities and the material wealth of the countries that hosted them, but had little to do with the practicalities of studying at a foreign university. This was confirmed by a student who interrupted a lengthy discussion I was having with some of his classmates about studying in the USA by saying: 'All want to go to America! And with this Facebook now, they see their friends who have gone driving a car after six months only and so they think: "Oh, then I also have to go."' Most of his peers, however, trusted the information they obtained through personal contacts, when, in fact, the picture generated through their online exchanges with young Nepalis in the diaspora was a highly partial and often unduly positive one.

The most visible and perhaps also the most forceful way in which information and images of studying abroad were spread in Kathmandu was through the marketing campaigns of international education consultancies. Along the city's main roads, gigantic billboards advertised foreign degrees and preparation courses for standardized tests. The daily newspapers published in Kathmandu often reserved entire pages for the announcements of international education fairs which promised 'free counselling and spot admission'. Even the walls of most buildings on campus were papered with flyers promoting preparation courses for the International English Language Testing System (IELTS) with a '6.5 guarantee', which was the test score commonly required by foreign immigration authorities as proof of sufficient English-language skills (see Figure 3.1).

Figure 3.1   Flyer of a Private Education Consultancy Displayed around Patan Campus, March 2012
Source: Author

At the time of my fieldwork, private agents that offered a variety of services, ranging from language test preparation courses to assistance with university admission and visa procedures, mushroomed across the city.

The students I met at Patan Campus had their reservations about the extent to which education consultants served as a reliable source of information. Talking about the emergence of this new service industry, Ameena and her friend, Dharana, mocked:

> Now if you walk along the road after every third or fourth house, there is a consultancy. 'Do you want to go abroad? No problem! Come to our consultancy!' [Dharana imitates a hawker and we burst out laughing]. First that urge came, like everybody suddenly wanted to go abroad. The consultancies saw they could make a profit out of this. So, now they are everywhere.

Nevertheless, Ameena, who grew up as the oldest daughter of a Newar family in a middle-class neighbourhood in Kathmandu, repeatedly expressed her interest in attending one of the international education fairs in Kathmandu. She argued: 'Women are treated differently [abroad]. Not like here, where there is no freedom for women. In other countries, women even enjoy going out at night. But here the families don't give permission and the security is also not good.'

Ameena and I were planning to go out together, but each time she had to cancel because she was unable to free up some extra time due to her domestic duties. She also felt discouraged by her boyfriend: 'He doesn't like the idea. He says that the girls who go to America are only good for guys who are already in America. But guys here are not interested in girls who go abroad.' When I met Ameena for the last time in March 2012, she remained resolute in her determination to experience herself what it was like to live in a Western country before she would marry and start a family in Nepal. However, she still had no idea about where or how to migrate.

Nischal, a 27-year-old Brahmin man, likewise, did not have any concrete plans of going abroad when we first met in October 2011. Yet, like many of his fellow students, he too aspired to apply for a student visa for a Western country and explained to me: 'The problem with Nepal is that we cannot use our education here. We train computer engineers when we need agriculturists. So even if you are educated and work your entire life, you still won't have enough money when you retire. That's why we rely on the opportunities offered by other countries.' After he learned that international students in Australia were permitted to work in parallel with their studies and were often granted permanent residency upon completing their courses, he was determined to apply for an Australian student visa. He calculated:

> No matter how hard I work, if I stay in Nepal, I will never be able to provide for my family. But my family is my first responsibility and in order to fulfil that I need to earn enough. Here, I will probably never earn more than Rs 20,000 per month. But abroad, you get paid in dollars, so it will easily be 1 lakh [Rs 100,000].

As the oldest son, Nischal bore financial responsibility for his mother and his two younger siblings. After the death of his father 10 years previously, the family had become heavily reliant on Nischal's income. Settling in a Western country was the best and perhaps the only way Nischal could imagine for himself to build a financially secure future. In response to his calculations of expected earnings, I advised him that living costs tended to be significantly higher in Australia than in Nepal and that students often only found low-wage work. Nischal frivolously dismissed any such concerns and asserted that it was acceptable for him to engage in a less prestigious job as a foreign student in Australia. At the same time, he categorically excluded any consideration of going abroad as a migrant worker. Labour migration, he argued, was associated with 'the 3D—dirty, dangerous, and difficult' and, hence, would jeopardize the social respect he had gained by being the first in his extended family to attain a university education.

When I met Nischal again in December 2011, he was hopeful to start the application process for an Australian student visa soon. His maternal uncle had agreed to loan him a substantial amount of money, so he had sufficient evidence of funds. In order to meet the language requirements, he had taken two test preparation courses, each costing Rs 3,000, and was following a third one offered by a different education consultancy. As a result, he knew everything about the separate sections of the standardized tests, the time limits, and the scoring systems, but he added in Nepali: 'I still can't say more than ABCD in English.' The English-language requirement had become the biggest obstacle for Nischal in his attempt to obtain a student visa.

Aware of the extent to which most of his fellow students on Patan Campus lacked the financial, social, or cultural capital needed to participate in international student mobility, one respondent noted with a sense of disillusion: 'People who are well qualified go abroad and so do the non-qualified ones. Only lower middle-class people, like us, stay here in Nepal.' With their richer peers going abroad as student migrants and their poorer peers going abroad as labour migrants, the young people I spoke with in Kathmandu were anxious about being left behind, removed from 'where things were happening' (cf. Jeffrey 2010b: 188). Their reliance on second-hand descriptions of life abroad only further reinforced highly desirable, but also highly diffuse, imaginaries of the foreign.

***

In conclusion, young Nepalis born in the 1980s are thought to be particularly well poised to take advantage of the newly emergent educational opportunities and occupational fields, which promise to offer better chances for increased levels of social and spatial mobility. In particular, the expansion of the Nepal's higher education sector has opened up new avenues for young people from different socio-spatial backgrounds to advance their social status. Liechty (2003) has observed that, in the 1990s, educational institutions, specifically private schools and university campuses, brought together young people from a range of caste, ethnic, and regional backgrounds, but he adds that 'Kathmandu's thousands of schools and campuses are physical spaces largely of, by, and for the middle class' (Liechty 2003: 264). However, in the 2010s, when I worked with university students of Patan Campus, university campuses were no longer the domain of the urban middle class. Instead, a growing number of young Nepalis belonging to social groups previously not represented at university level are now obtaining academic qualifications (cf. Faye 2017; Valentin 2011).

Precisely because these changes are (yet) less visible from a macro perspective, I found it useful to explore in depth how exactly young people's aspirations for social mobility are reflected in everyday forms of spatial mobility. Among researchers working on topics related to student mobilities, it is well established that the very process of relocating to a different place forms an integral part of young people's learning and often implies an upward move-ment along the social hierarchy (for example, Findlay et al. 2012;

Holdsworth 2009; Waters 2006, 2012). While existing literature on student mobilities has primarily centred on long-distance migration, the empirical findings presented in this chapter suggest that young people are able to maintain and nurture their social standing as an educated person through various forms of mobilities, including the daily commute to campus, virtual travels, and even small bodily gestures. At the same time, my findings support the idea that spatial strategies for social ascent tend to be 'anti-local', in the sense that it is commonly thought to be necessary for young people to leave their homes in order to take advantage of presumably better educational opportunities available elsewhere (see also Holloway and Pimlott-Wilson 2011).

Related to this, my analysis furthermore makes evident that young people's participation in higher education forms an integral part of a wider identity-making project. This is of particular importance for the growing number of students from social groups that previously had been discriminated against because of their caste, gender, or geographical origin. The friendships and social networks these young people build on campus help them in their attempts to reposition themselves in wider society. The very experience of being liked and respected by their peers gives these young people some confidence in their capacity to overcome social boundaries around which the lives of previous generations of Nepalis had been structured.

In conversations about their educational trajectories, the students I spoke with commonly referred to their parents, relatives, peers, and other members of their own communities. These social influences provide important points of reference for them, and often open up new opportunities, which otherwise would have been inaccessible or even unthinkable for these young people. At the same time, the hopes which parents attach to their children's educational attainments do not necessarily correspond to the ideas young people obtain from their friends or through online interactions. Consequently, it could be challenging for young people to negotiate these different social influences and to decide which educational and occupational pathway they want to follow.

More specifically, it is apparent that socially instilled aspirations for a lucrative career or an international education generally stand in stark contrast to the practicable avenues available to the majority of university students in urban Nepal. The prestige attached to a university education does not necessarily allow for a successful transition into the modern labour market. In this respect, it is particularly disconcerting for the young Nepalis I spoke with that their parents' high-rising hopes and expectations seemed to take little account of the realities of present-day life in Kathmandu. I therefore argue that Appadurai's (2004) conceptualization of the capacity to aspire as a basis for social ascent needs to be revised as it risks downplaying important counterforces. Instead, I have sought to think through young people's narratives about their potential futures in terms of both aspiration as well as apprehension (see also Smith 2013). By paying equal attention to the possibilities and the constraints that young people anticipate for the future, I have been able to identify a number of influences that may delimit young people's horizons of opportunity and obstruct their attempts to realize the hope for a more prosperous future.

Another reason for the students of Patan Campus to feel anxious with regard to the future is the extent to which most of them appeared to be unable to follow the educational routes taken by their more affluent peers. Unable to draw from the economic, social, and cultural resources required to participate in international student mobility, they are largely dependent on second-hand information about life abroad. Their daily encounters with images of and stories about their peers studying at universities in other countries have generated overly positive imaginaries, with the result that potential risks involved in studying and living in a foreign country have been blinded out and 'studying abroad' has become an end in itself. Such findings illustrate well that, in an interconnected world, even those who do not physically move are no less affected by enhanced levels of mobility than their migrating peers. This also epitomizes the extent to which dominant discourses, according to which education-related mobility is predominately ascribed with positive meanings, can backfire. Rather than serving as an inspiration, such prevalent associations and related social expectations may leave young people with a sense of unresolvedness: hopeful to move above their social origins and, at the same time, anxious to continue lagging behind upper-status groups.

4

Confronting the Present

Students' Absence from and Presence on Campus

On my first day on campus, I was accompanied by Dhirendra, a member of the student union. We had been introduced to one another by a mutual friend a few days earlier and Dhirendra had agreed to show me around the campus, as well as introduce me to his peers and the administrative staff. I followed him around the campus, constantly stopping to greet lecturers and shake hands with students. Later that week, Dhirendra also took me to the office of the vice president—though only after I had repeatedly requested him to do so, since he did not seem to attach much importance to an official introduction. I explained my intent to the vice president of the campus who asked me to submit a formal application letter. Before I could explain that I would bring the necessary documents the following day, the vice president ripped out a blank page from a notebook lying on the desk in front of him and gave it to Dhirendra, who wrote the place and date on top of the page and asked me to add a sentence about my research topic along with my signature. I did as I was told. Dhirendra then passed the paper back to the vice president and said that it was okay and my request was approved.[1]

[1] This 'application procedure' should not be mistaken for my official application for a research permit, in the course of which I registered with

As a member of the student union, Dhirendra was perceived to be in a powerful position. This was made clear to me on my first day on campus when I explained to a group of students that I felt uneasy to start my research project without having informed the head of the campus administration or his deputy. In response, the students told me that I had already met 'the chief of the campus' and, hence, should not be too worried about being formally introduced to the campus administration. Dhirendra was a vital gatekeeper and a very resourceful contact person without whom it would have been much more difficult for me to commence my research project. He had grown up as the eldest son of a Tamang family in a small town at the rim of the Kathmandu Valley. At the time of my field research, he was in his early thirties and enrolled in the master's programme at the sociology department. He had already completed his intermediate and his bachelor's studies at Patan Campus. Yet, only on one occasion during the entire nine months that I came to campus on a daily basis, Dhirendra joined me to attend a lecture in sociology. He came unprepared and asked me for a pen and paper. He gave up taking notes after 10 minutes and left soon after. Most of the time, I found Dhirendra sitting by the tea stalls playing chess.

Unlike the vast majority of public university students, Dhirendra did not have a paid job and, therefore, spent most of the day on and around the campus. The apartment where he lived, together with his four siblings, was only a 5-minute walk from the campus. Those of his peers whom he occasionally invited for tea to his place mentioned to me that they did not understand how he was able to afford the rent for a 5–room, fully furnished apartment in this neighbourhood. Asked about his tasks and responsibilities as a member of the student union, Dhirendra told me: 'We are in charge of the distribution of funds that we receive from the college administration for student welfare. For special occasions, we also raise additional funds from students.' I was told by several students that for the organization of the campus sports day, which took place in December 2011, the student union had asked for Rs 20 lakh (more than

---

the Centre of International Relations at Tribhuvan University and obtained approval for my research project from the MoE and the Department of Immigration.

US$ 17,000) from the campus administration and required each participant to pay an extra Rs 50. The campus sports day primarily entailed a running competition for which a police escort had been arranged and all participants had been equipped with red headbands and flags showing the emblem of the student wing affiliated with the Communist Party of Nepal (Unified Marxist–Leninist). Based on these observations, it appeared to be unlikely that the funds were used exclusively for the sports day, which, in any case, served primarily as a political campaign for Dhirendra and his supporters (see Figure 4.1).

By the end of the year, rumours that the student union elections would be held in February or March 2012 intensified. Dhirendra very much welcomed the news and explained to me: 'The elections are long overdue. If there will be elections on campus, somebody else can replace me in the student union and I can be promoted into a position at national level or so. Without the elections, we are just here waiting.' Besides the campus sports day, several other events were organized during those weeks, including the freshers'

Figure 4.1 Runners at the Starting Line during the Campus Sports Day, December 2011
Source: Author

induction programme, a picnic, a quiz, and vacation courses during the semester break in January. All of these events appeared to be fun activities for students to socialize outside the classrooms but, in fact, each of them was repurposed by different student organizations for their political campaigns. It was at this stage that Dhirendra's friends repeatedly requested me to introduce Dhirendra to my research participants, especially those who were studying for a degree in humanities and social sciences. Only then did I learn that, whereas other departments did not limit the number of admissions, the natural sciences department admitted a maximum of 180 students per year, out of which 40 slots were allocated by the student union. 'This is why all the physics students are anyway behind Dhirendra. But we need your help to reach students from the other departments', one of Dhirendra's supporters told me bluntly. From the very beginning, I had been acutely aware that it would be a challenge for me to maintain a neutral stand with regard to party politics and keep any information shared with me strictly confidential. I managed to do so by maintaining a cordial but sporadic contact with Dhirendra and other student politicians, with the result that the rest of the students did not directly associate me with any of the political student organizations.

Even though only a small minority of students were actively involved in party politics, student politicians were certainly the most visible subgroup among the student community. This became particularly evident to me when reading the local newspapers. The local media apparently was most likely to report about public university students whenever a protest or a strike took place. Some of the articles about Tribhuvan University and its constituent campuses that I collected over the course of my research bore the following headlines:

'TU Students Boycott BBS Exams' (*eKantipur*, January 14, 2010).
'TU Mgmt Dept Padlocked' (*eKantipur*, March 28, 2010).
'Students Protest Fuel Price Hike' (*The Himalayan Times*, March 10, 2012).
'Students Protest Tuition Fee Hike' (*eKantipur*, September 24, 2012).
'Students Protest Re-exam after Question Leak' (*Republica*, September 26, 2012).
'Getting on TU Protest Bandwagon' (*The Kathmandu Post*, December 26, 2012).

'Valley Traffic Impeded Following Students' Protest' (*The Himalayan Times*, March 21, 2013).
'MBBS Students on the Warpath' (*The Kathmandu Post*, June 28, 2013)
'NSU [Nepal Student Union] Stages Sit-in at TU' (*Republica*, June 4, 2013).

Nepal has had a long history of student politics and mass protest movements (Snellinger 2005). In the aftermath of the civil war, however, street protests and strikes of varying scales and impacts emerged as the most widespread means of expressing collective disagreement. Considering that in 2010 alone, 1,205 events related to general strikes were reported across the whole country, some local observers have arrived at the conclusion that in the absence of a constitution and good governance, Nepali society has developed a '*bandh* culture' (Shrestha and Chaudhary 2013). The Nepali and Hindi word 'bandh' means 'closed' or 'shut' in English. It is commonly used to describe a general strike due to which private businesses or public institutions, including schools and colleges, are forced to remain closed and vehicular traffic and public transport often comes to a complete stop, leaving the roads largely deserted. In recent years, various interest groups, ranging from journalists to slum dwellers, have resorted to street protests to make public their specific demands. However, the most effective strikes that bring public life to a complete halt are still those that are called by the national political parties and their respective youth wings. Consequently, often it is politically active students who are seen standing at the forefront of such public remonstrations (see also Snellinger 2010). The majority of people I met in Kathmandu, however, agreed that the costs of such frequent interruptions of daily life fell most heavily on ordinary residents. Most of them, therefore, were utterly annoyed by the seemingly never-ending political agitations and by young people's involvement in party politics.

More than feeling irritated, some of the students I spoke with felt even threatened by student politics as they recalled having witnessed a number of instances where disagreements between rival student organizations had escalated into vandalism and fights on campus. Memories of previous violent clashes were still visible on campus: the glass of most classroom windows facing the main street leading up to Patan

Dhoka was shattered. I was told that neither the campus administration nor the student union was willing to repair the damage because another student protest was sure to happen. Following such aggressive incidents, it sometimes took as little as a rumour about an apparent disagreement between political student activists for police forces to arrive in large numbers on the campus and patrol the premises. I was warned that once the elections drew closer, the overwhelming majority of students would no longer come to campus because it was considered to be unsafe. The few who still came to campus would do so not to attend classes but to participate in election campaigns. In the end, the Free Students Union elections were called off in February 2012 over a dispute about whether to use a first-past-the-post or proportional representation system. Nevertheless, the tensions and anxieties which built up in anticipation of the elections to be held underline that young people's collective impact can play out in destructive ways and that youth agency can have a negative connotation.

***

I got to know Anandi, aged 25 in 2011, as a very amiable and obliging young woman. She, together with her younger sister and brother, had been brought up in an upper-caste Newar family in the old town centre of Patan. Anandi's father had completed tenth grade and worked as a lower-level government officer. Her mother had acquired some literacy skills without ever attaining formal schooling and ran a small retail store, selling everything from stationeries to pastries. For Anandi, her family's well-being was a key priority in life:

> I am the eldest in the house. Therefore, it is my responsibility to give right guidance to my brother and sister. I also have to do what my parents expect from me. I think it is important to do something here. It is my responsibility and my wish to support my family and to take care of the things that I have to do after marriage. These things are important, because they are related to family.

Anandi's daily routine was organized around family life. She usually got up at 5:00 a.m. to go to the temple for morning puja (religious offerings). Then she came back and made tea for her father. Afterwards, she went to the campus and returned home at around

10:30 a.m. to prepare some food and attend to other chores in the house. In the afternoon, she had time to study before her younger brother came home from school at 3:00 p.m. They ate together, and then Anandi went to help her mother in the store. She would normally go back to the house to start preparing the dinner at around 6:00 p.m. By the time she finished her household duties, it was usually 10:00 p.m. Before going to sleep, Anandi tried to spend some more time preparing for the lectures the following day.

During her bachelor's studies, Anandi initially used to work as a primary schoolteacher. However, after she failed the first-year examinations in mathematics, she decided to leave the job and concentrate on her education alongside her domestic duties. In addition, she changed to a course at the social sciences department in the hope that it would be easier and less time-consuming to prepare for the exams. Even though she continued to study sociology at master's level, she was not entirely happy with her choice of subject:

> I could not decide whether to take economics or sociology, even though I thought about the pros and cons for a very long time. Eventually, I took sociology thinking that it would go smoothly if I took an easy subject. But now I regret that I did not decide for a difficult subject. It would have been better for my family.

According to Anandi, her individual efforts to succeed in a supposedly more difficult subject would have rebounded to the social standing of her entire family.

In Nepali society, and perhaps even more so among upper castes (Cameron 1998; Rankin 2003), the social respectability of women is held particularly high. Any kind of behaviour considered to be inappropriate for a woman may jeopardize the arrangement of a favourable marriage, which, in turn, would undermine the social prestige of the whole family and may, in the worst case, lead to being prohibited from entering the house of the family (Subedi 1999: 128; see also Lind Petersen 2011: 121). Sumita, a 23-year-old Brahmin woman, who, in 2011, like Anandi, was unmarried and living with her parents in Kathmandu, told me in this context:

> In the past, families gave priority to the sons' education. But now, girls and boys are treated equally. That is because in the past, boys

used to marry illiterate girls, even though boys were more educated. But now, boys want girls of the same educational level. They demand girls according to their level. Like, in my case, if I would have married when I was in my teens, I would probably have got married to just any kind of guy.... Now I am studying at master's level. I won't marry a boy studying at +2! Nobody does!

None of the educated young women I met on Patan Campus seriously challenged their role as a future wife and daughter-in-law. However, they hoped that their educational attainments would allow them to gain the respect not only of their natal family but also their future in-laws. Most of the female students I spoke with therefore told me that they did not want to marry before finishing their master's degree.

Those few who were already married at the time of my field research agreed that it was challenging to reconcile their role and responsibilities as a young wife with their studies. Roshni's parents had arranged for her marriage just as she finished her bachelor's studies in 2005. She explained to me: 'It was a matter of honour [*ijjat*] for my family and also for my husband's family. They are quite traditional and not much educated.' Roshni grew up as the older of two daughters in an upper-caste family in the northern part of Kathmandu and had moved in with her husband's family after the wedding. Nobody in her extended family held a university degree. Roshni's husband had dropped out in grade 11, before completing the intermediate level. Initially, he did not understand why Roshni wanted to continue her education. 'My husband kept saying: "Why do you have to study? You already have studied enough and now you will not have the time." [pause] But I am stubborn!', she added with a bright and confident smile. At the age of 29, three years after she got married, Roshni returned to university and enrolled for a master's in management and commerce at Patan Campus.

Roshni's day usually began before 4:00 a.m. and ended after 10:00 p.m. Her mother-in-law expected her to cook a full meal for the family twice a day. Her husband's income as a salesman did not suffice to cover their cost of living, so Roshni also worked five days a week as a teacher for a private school. Nonetheless, she tried to go to the campus every day and attended her classes regularly. When I asked her how she was able to handle all the competing priorities, she replied:

> It's not because I am thinking of a particular job or a particular position. I just do it for myself. The campus is the place where we can meet our friends and talk to different people. Otherwise, there is no time for that. Only when I started university, I learned how to interact with different people and I developed my own opinions. I have changed a lot in this way. If I had not studied, I would not be the person I am today.

According to Roshni, learning did not only take place inside the classrooms but also outside on the campus premises through the many conversations she had with fellow students and friends.

For the very same reason, going to campus constituted a fixed part of Anandi's daily schedule too, even though she showed much less interest in her studies. Every day, she arrived on campus just before classes started at 6:30 a.m. and returned home immediately after classes finished between 9:30 a.m. and 10:00 a.m. During this time, however, I usually found her by the tea stalls chatting with friends rather than inside the classroom. It was so common for students to skip classes though they were physically present on, or at least around, campus that the—not entirely correct—English term 'bunking classes' had become part of the Nepali vocabulary. It was telling that the tea stalls tended to be packed with students during class hours and vacated after classes had finished. When I asked Anandi why she continued going to campus without actually following her course, she explained to me: 'I have to come to campus in the morning. Otherwise, my parents will think I am not studying well. For them, education is the first priority. They are so happy now that my sister is a college topper. But I find no satisfaction in studying…. Still, I just need to clear it [the master's degree] somehow.'

Anandi's younger sister had successfully completed a medical degree at the teaching hospital in Kathmandu and, in 2011, had started to work at a hospital that specialized in the treatment of cancer. Anandi appreciated that her sister had brought great honour to the family. At the same time, her sister's success seemed to put Anandi under more pressure. While she was not enthusiastic about her university studies, she was also afraid of disappointing her parents. For this reason, Anandi was careful not to jeopardize her reputation as a respectable educated woman, which also meant that there was little opportunity for her to hang out with friends in public. By going to campus in the morning, Anandi could meet her friends and, simultaneously, maintain the image of the diligent student that her parents expected her to be.

***

When I first met Rohan in September 2011, I was surprised to find out that he was a public university student. I was having lunch in a small eatery in a part of the city where several international organizations and national NGOs had their offices. I knew from other research participants that most students considered this neighbourhood relatively pricey. I, therefore, had not expected to meet any of them there. Rohan was sitting across the table from me, eating a bowl of *thukpa* (spicy noodle soup), while I was taking down notes on my visit to the campus earlier that morning. Suspecting that I was not a tourist, Rohan was curious to find out what I was doing in Nepal. He laughed when I told him about my research project with students from Patan Campus and explained that I could as well interview him. In 2011, Rohan was enrolled for the second year of the master's programme in sociology at Patan Campus.

It quickly became part of my routine in Kathmandu to meet with Rohan during his lunch break once a week. Born in 1987, he had grown up in Kathmandu in an upper-caste family. He worked in an office building nearby, for an organization which assisted children from unprivileged backgrounds, including street children and children of squatters, to attain basic levels of education. He wanted to continue his career in the development sector and, ideally, work for a United Nations (UN) agency in the future. Rohan knew that it would be difficult to secure a post in this highly competitive job market and felt that he needed both academic credentials and at least 3–5 years of work experience to stand a chance. He gave the example of his supervisor, who held an MA degree in sociology from Patan Campus and a second MA degree in economics from Shanker Dev Campus and had been offered funding from Kathmandu University for her doctoral studies. She had founded the organization while she was studying at master's level and, with her work, had earned a good reputation as an educationist in the development sector. For Rohan, this woman was an important role model and he regularly sought her advice about course contents, exam preparations, and career choices.

Rohan's family could only offer limited support in this respect. His mother had acquired basic literacy skills and his father had dropped out of secondary school. His parents ran a small grocery store which, in previous years, had generated an income sufficient to cover the family's living expenses. More recently, however, the rent for the small retail space had gone up steeply, with the result that his parents were no longer able to help Rohan pay for university. Only because Rohan succeeded in securing a paid job during his bachelor's degree could he continue his studies. Rohan was disappointed that his younger sister was apparently less committed to obtaining a university degree. She had difficulty in passing a mandatory course in English and had dropped out of the bachelor's programme. Rohan seemed to take it personally that his sister had decided to discontinue her studies before completing a university degree, even though he had offered to help.

When asked about his own studies, Rohan answered: 'I believe in a proverb that we have in Nepali. It says that your education ends when your life ends.' He went on to explain that he spend at least three hours every evening to prepare for the exams. He intended to complete his coursework during the academic year 2011–12 and had started to explore possible topics for his master's thesis. Despite expressing much interest in his subject, Rohan barely ever went to the campus. He explained to me that he only went to the campus to pay his fees and to pick up his student identification card that permitted him access to the examination hall on the day of final exams. In the same manner, he had already completed his bachelor's degree in sociology and English. Self-consciously, he identified himself as a 'tourist student': 'Tourists go to see places, just out of curiosity, but without really knowing much about them. So, that's why I am a tourist student, because I don't know the people on campus and only go there once in a while when there is nothing better to do.' Instead of going to the campus himself, Rohan requested me to enquire about the deadline for submitting a thesis outline, to check for the course companion for sociology in the bookstores located next to the campus, and to find out whether last year's exam results were finally published. Since he did not know any of his fellow classmates, I was the closest connection Rohan had with Patan Campus.

When I asked the head of the sociology department at Patan Campus about the number of students enrolled for the master's programme before the mid-term break in January 2012, she explained that more than 200 students had registered at the beginning of the academic year 2011–12, but no more than 35 students usually sat in her lectures. The proportions were no different at the central departments of Tribhuvan University, as I was told by a faculty member. He showed me enrolment records of the previous academic year according to which 1,100 students had been admitted to study for a degree in sociology; however, only 10 per cent had regularly attended the classes. Most lecturers I spoke with were very understanding of students' lack of attendance and reasoned that the majority of students were 'studying by working'. In order to accommodate the students' need to work full time alongside their university studies, most lectures on Patan Campus were scheduled between 6:30 a.m. and 10:00 a.m. to fit around official working hours.

In contrast, the students I spoke with felt that it was a waste of time to travel to the campus early in the morning before work only to find out that classes had been cancelled again. They often joked that the campus functioned based on a 'helmet faculty', since lecturers had to rush on their motorbikes from one college to another without having time to take off their helmets during class. In order to make ends meet, the majority of faculty members indeed worked two or three additional shifts at private colleges, with the result that they often turned up late for class or not at all. Records kept by Tribhuvan University show that, during the academic year 2011–12, only half of the required 150 class sessions per year were conducted on most of the constituent campuses belonging to the TU system.

One Sunday in November 2011, Rohan called to say that he was on campus to pay his registration fees. I found him waiting in line in front of the admissions office and he greeted me by saying in a hushed voice: 'Even on a Sunday, when we don't have to go to work,

we don't attend the lectures. Look, all the students are standing outside enjoying the sun. It only confirms that it's not worth my time
to come here more regularly.' Once we walked away from the other
students, Rohan continued to explain to me that most high-ranked
politicians were former student leaders. He believed that many students hung out on campus because they wanted to get involved in
party politics and hoped to use their connections to secure a job
with the government. Rohan complained:

> The problem with this is that the student organizations have so much
> power and close down the campus whenever there is a political con-
> flict at the national level. They call it the 'youth force'. But every-
> thing in Nepal is delayed in this way. They said it would take two
> years for the new constitution. Already five years have passed and who
> knows when it will be finalized! And in all these years, our exams have
> been postponed for more than six months. So, I already lost one year
> during my master's. But the student union doesn't care whether the
> schedule is interrupted or not. That's why I don't like going to cam-
> pus. It is so politicized. People might think I am getting involved with
> these student politicians and that I got on the wrong track.

In terms of his social background, Rohan had indeed much in
common with some of the student politicians. Most of the members
of the student union were high-caste, middle-class, young men (see
also Snellinger 2018). This highly visible subgroup of university
students certainly influenced how university students in general,
and specifically those with similar characteristics, were perceived by
wider society. In order to avoid any potentially negative associations,
Rohan refrained from going to campus regularly and preferred to
rely on autodidactic methods to obtain a graduate degree.

On a Wednesday in late December 2011, university campuses,
schools, offices, stores, and other public institutions were closed
for the second day in a row due to a bandh. For a change, Rohan
and I enjoyed walking along one of the main roads as the absence
of motorized vehicles had significantly eased the otherwise severe
noise and air pollution. As I was marvelling at the panoramic
view of the Himalayas, which was usually concealed by thick
smog, Rohan stopped and remarked: 'The problem of our generation is that we don't have a schedule—well, apart from the

load-shedding schedule.' The term 'load-shedding' is used to refer to the planned power cuts that the Nepal Electricity Authority imposes in order to cope with mismatched supply and demand, and that are published in the form of a weekly schedule in all daily newspapers. As Nepal almost exclusively relies on hydropower, scheduled power cuts usually add up to more than 15 hours a day during the dry season from October through March. Political instabilities, historically rooted conflicts of interests between different stakeholders, and inefficient management have hindered attempts to find an appropriate solution for Nepal's electricity crisis (Shrestha 2010). The idea that the load-shedding schedule—the epitome of the country's incessant economic and political problems—seemed to be the only constant that made daily life in Kathmandu somewhat projectable illustrates just too well how difficult it was for aspirational young Nepalis like Rohan to progress smoothly through the formal education system and realize their educational and professional ambitions.

***

In line with other human geographers interested in the ways in which young people appropriate and use certain spaces of everyday lives, I found that the campus constituted a kind of spatial separation of the younger generation from the older (see, for example, Hopkins and Pain 2007; Vanderbeck 2007). The campus was a place removed from young people's places of residence. More importantly perhaps, the parental generation had a severely limited understanding of what it means to study at university as the large majority of them had not attained higher levels of education and, in fact, had never been inside a university building. In this respect, the weight of evidence suggests that the daily routines of the young Nepalis I met on Patan Campus were markedly different than those of their parents.

A unilateral focus on these generational differences, however, runs the risk of overlooking a number of values and norms which continue to be passed on from one generation to the next. In particular, notions of female and male respectability upheld by the parental generation still served as crucial points of reference against which young people's performance was being judged. At the same time, established life trajectories specific to people's gender, caste, and ethnicity had become obscured. Thus, it appeared to be no longer sufficient for Nepal's younger population to primarily reproduce the life paths and achievements of previous generations. Those seen to belong to the newly educated generation were expected to pursue higher goals and identify new ways of being, in order to realize the hope of a socially successful and financially secure future life.

To this end, I hold that young people's educational experiences and the decisions they made in relation to their educational careers were, to a large extent, the product of a multitude of social influences that press down on young people as they move through the formal education system. In this context, I found it useful to think through specific decision-making situations that young Nepalis had to negotiate with regard to their studies at university as sites of vital conjunctures: 'socially structured zones of possibility that emerge around specific periods of potential transformation in a life' (Johnson-Hanks 2002: 871). The university campus played a particularly important role in this respect as educated young Nepalis were anxious to trace how they compared to their peers. Such comparisons revealed much about their chances of gaining social respect.

Over the course of my research on Patan Campus, it became apparent that students were acutely aware of how their absence from or presence on campus could reflect back on them. The physical space of the campus was ascribed with value-laden images and meanings, which were directly projected onto the identities of the individual students. On the one hand, the campus represented an important space around which students' daily routines were structured and which allowed them to distinguish themselves from the parental generation and their less educated peers. Going to campus was closely associated with a host of social values attached to higher levels of education and, in this sense, stood for an honourable status. On the other hand, many people in Nepal had come to think of public university campuses as microcosms of national party rivalries. This specific perception had become manifested in the social consciousness in the light of reports in the local media about seemingly never-ending political agitations and on the basis of certain practices associated with one of the most visible subgroups of public university students, namely, politically active students. As a result, students of Patan Campus and other public university campuses in Kathmandu often found themselves confronted with rather broad-brush generalizations, which took little account of their individual performance and attitudes.

The majority of the young people I spoke with successfully negotiated such dominant but often overly simplistic representations and managed to elude potential controversies about their social reputation. Some young men, for example, decided against hanging out on campus in recognition of commonly held perceptions according to which the university campus was seen to offer a particularly suitable environment for political actors to reach out to educated young people and mobilize them for their own interests. By contrast, female students used the university campus as a place to meet and interact with their friends. Most of the young women I spoke with agreed that it was generally unacceptable for them to socialize with peers, especially young men, in public. The university campus, however, provided a space where young women were somewhat removed from the supervision of their families and where they could simultaneously nurture their social standing as an educated person. In this sense, the university campus was more than an educational institution in its conventional sense. For the young Nepalis I spoke with, the campus provided a multifunctional space of learning, where they could gain new ideas not only (and perhaps not even primarily) inside the classrooms but also through friendships and informal interactions with their peers.

By framing certain decision-making situations as vital conjunctures, it becomes possible to grasp this curious combination of social pressures that bear down hard on young people but, simultaneously, open up new opportunities for them to develop a sense of agency. In this chapter, I have shown that an analysis of young people's spatial practices on and around the campus can reveal much about the meanings and ideas associated with certain spaces of their everyday lives and the ways in which young people try to comply with established notions of social respectability in an attempt to forge a future for themselves and their families. In this way, a focus on their spatial practices and underlying motivations can advance our understanding of how young people experience and navigate sites of vital conjunctures.

5

Putting Down Roots to Move On

Students' Modest Appropriations of Dominant
Future Strategies

In 2002, the *Nepali Times* published an article, 'A Nation's Call',
about 'the cream of the nation's student crop' which left Nepal in
order to attain higher education and, eventually, settle in Europe,
Australia, Canada, and, particularly, the US (Sherpa 2002).
According to the author, this was a matter of urgency as the cost of
this 'brain drain' was to weigh heavily on the country's potential for
economic growth. To lend weight to his point, the author compared
Nepali student migrants with Aniko, the famous artist who was
born in the thirteenth century in the Kathmandu Valley but spent
his most productive life phase at the court of an emperor in China
without ever returning to his place of origin. Ten years later—at
the time of my field research—the tone of the debate on foreign
migration in Nepali popular media remained much the same. Young
emigrants from Nepal were continuously called upon to 'return to
the home country for good' and to 'convert brain drain into brain
gain' (*Republica* 2012).

The students I met in Kathmandu resented this line of argumen-
tation. In the face of growing dependence of the country's economy
on remittances and the run for foreign degrees, nobody seemed to

pay much attention to their educational achievements or appreciated their efforts to map out promising future pathways in Nepal. For example, Narendra, aged 24 in 2012, remarked with a sense of dismay:

> I told you about the school building project we did in the village. We raised a lot of funds and gave to that school. And that was really a motivation. But our relatives or the people that know us, they just blame you sometimes: 'You are not going abroad?!' So what? I am not going abroad. It doesn't mean that I am not doing anything over here. I have been doing these kinds of things over here and your son and daughter are there in the US. What are they doing for the society?

Narendra and I were having lunch at his home after he had taken me on his motorbike around the area of Boudha to show me his family's business and the office where he worked. Narendra's family was part of the new propertied urban class. His two older brothers had set up a lucrative thangka painting business in Kathmandu. Many of the traditional Buddhist artworks that were produced in the workshop sold for over US$ 1,000 in the international market. The family had invested the money partly in the construction of a new four-storeyed house located in an upmarket residential neighbourhood and, to a large extent, also in Narendra's education. Narendra had attended a highly reputable private school and held a bachelor's degree from Kathmandu's private university. His family was extremely proud of him. Upon entering the house, I had noticed that the walls of the living room were fully decorated with photographs showing Narendra in his graduation gown and with his bachelor's certificate in his hands. Unable to hide his slight embarrassment, Narendra had joked that his pictures were more prominently displayed in the house than the paintings of Buddhist deities.

When we had talked about his educational background before, Narendra had told me that they were all together 60 students in his undergraduate programme but only seven, including himself, were still in Nepal a year following their graduation. Everybody else had moved abroad to continue their academic education at universities in North America, Europe, and Australia. As we sat at the table having lunch, I asked him about a pile of books that was lying next to us and included the *The Official Guide to the TOEFL Test* and *GRE Prep*.[1] Narendra shook his head and replied:

> Ever since I completed my bachelor's degree, my family has been asking: 'Why don't you just go and apply for a student visa? You should go to the US!' But I always tried to resist myself. But the problem is, if I don't go, we have neighbours and his son or daughter might go abroad and he will send a picture, like sitting in a car. Again, my mom or brother will feel jealous, isn't it? 'See he has already gone.' And then he will send a new cell phone, iPhone, to his family: 'See he is sending this, and you are sitting here'. That kind of thing. And for that, in order to resist that society or that talking, it is not that easy.

The decision to move abroad in pursuit of an international education often constituted a joint family project. The moment a son or a daughter left Nepal on a student visa to a Western country, the entire family seemed to gain in social prestige. The specific type of the higher education institution or the individual performance of the student made no difference in this respect. In the conversation I had with Narendra, it became apparent that this kind of overvaluation of a Western education frustrated him, not least because it led to tensions within his family. He told me:

> Actually the problem is, the generation before us is not very educated. So, they even don't know what their son or daughter is doing abroad. Most of them who go to the US just go for the community college and even that certificate, sometimes, is not even valid. Those who go to Australia just go for the vocational training, not even academic course. And our family members don't know about these things. They just say: 'You know, my son is there in Australia and he is now applying for the PR [permanent residency].' And that's the difficult thing. They do not understand.

Most of the students I met on Patan Campus shared this sense of resentment, which also reflected in a popular joke that I was

---

[1] The Graduate Record Examinations (GRE) and the Test of English as a Foreign Language (TOEFL) are standardized tests that are part of the admission requirements of most universities in the US.

repeatedly told and ran along the following line: 'Even a goat coming from America would be married to a good girl.'

Several weeks before we had this conversation, the head of the economics department at Patan Campus had introduced me to Narendra during a panel discussion hosted by the department. Together with other students and lecturers, Narendra had organized the event and had invited some high-level employees of the Central Bank of Nepal to talk about the government's newly published economic report. The event was well received by the campus administration and the students, who frequently complained to me that their study programmes offered no opportunities for discussions and networking. At the same time, it was a rather heated debate as most of the questions from the audience were about the government's failure to provide better job opportunities for educated young people. Narendra was standing next to me in the back of the room and commented on the discussion by saying in English to me: 'People are good in blaming others for not getting any opportunities. But when you point the finger at others [makes the gesture with his hand], three fingers are pointing back at you.'

When we later sat together in a coffee shop, I followed up on his remark and he replied: 'I think we also need to take responsibility ourselves. Government cannot do everything. Even we citizens should work for ourselves! But everybody is always just blaming the government. Always! For not getting [any job opportunities]. Why don't they give something themselves?' He moved on to explain how he had successfully established an NGO through which he and his small team initiated and supported school-building projects in rural areas of eastern Nepal. In fact, though Narendra had spent his entire life in Kathmandu, his grandparents were originally from a small Tamang village located 80 km east of the Kathmandu Valley in Ramecchap district. Narendra maintained close ties with the village community and proudly told me that his efforts to raise funds for the construction of the school had earned him the respect of the village community.

When I met Narendra for the last time in March 2012, he had been made an offer to assist with a feasibility study for a development project funded by the UK government in Ramecchap district. He had come to an agreement with his family that he would not start to apply for the admission and visa process before he earned his master's degree from Patan Campus and implemented his plans to add a library building to the school in the village. Although he had not entirely forgone the idea of applying to a university in the US, staying in Nepal was still his preferred option. He emphasized: 'Going abroad means struggling in some other country. But we can also do it from here in a more "feel proud" way.'

***

On a sunny Saturday in November 2011, I joined 600 volunteers to spend the day cleaning the premises of a children's hospital in Kathmandu. A group of students who were enrolled for the master's programme in sociology on Patan Campus had asked me to come along. When we arrived at the site, we found Jeevan, a 27-year-old Dalit man, standing on a chair in front of a crowd of predominately young people, all equipped with brooms, rubber cloves, and surgical masks, waiting for him to give further instructions (see Figure 5.1).

Figure 5.1 Students Volunteering to Clean a Children's Hospital in Kathmandu, November 2011
Source: Author

Behind him hung a large banner which read in English: 'If not we, then who? If not now, then when?' Jeevan was happy to see that so many of his classmates had come to support the campaign, which he had organized in his capacity as a co-founder of an organization called 'Volunteer for Change'. As I was sweeping the corridors of the hospital, I learned that Jeevan, together with his friends, had managed to mobilize students from a range of different private and public colleges who felt motivated to spend their spare time for this voluntary initiative because 'this was a way in which everybody could contribute at least a little bit and bring about change', one of my fellow cleaners explained to me.

Jeevan and his peers belonged to a generation of Nepalis who had been told throughout their young lives that young people's resourcefulness offered an answer to the country's persisting economic, political, and social problems. During their schooldays in the 1990s, discourses about modernization and development of the country found a strong articulation in the national school curriculum (for example, Pigg 1992; Skinner and Holland 1996). Children's textbooks included images of young people engaged in various social initiatives, such as planting trees or cleaning a temple courtyard (Caddell 2007; Gellner 2004). The international donor institutions that supported the development and publication of school materials also left their mark by including issues related to children's rights, poverty reduction, health, and environmental protection in the national school curriculum (Caddell 2007: 275). The 'educated' person came to be seen as somebody who was well behaved, served the country's development, and held a salaried job (Skinner and Holland 1996; Valentin 2005).

In the aftermath of the civil war, national leaders and international actors involved in processes of peace building and planned development reinvigorated the vision of youth as a source of hope for a more prosperous and socially just future. The National Youth Policy, published in 2010 and legally enacted in 2015, described the country's newly educated younger population as 'pioneers of economic, social, political, and culture transformations' and 'an important asset of the nation' because of moral fibres, such as, courage, innovativeness, inquisitiveness, and self-confidence (MoYS 2010). With the World Bank (2007) being one of the strongest proponents of youth entrepreneurship, numerous not-for-profit organizations, international donor agencies, and private businesses instigated a series of programmes encouraging young people to develop and implement innovative solutions for the challenges faced by Nepali society. In 2011, for example, the country's largest private sector enterprise, Surya Nepal, launched an award for social entrepreneurship with the aim to celebrate 'Nepal's change agents' and to inspire young people to become 'job creators' instead of 'job seekers'.[2] Many youth-directed policies implied that it was only a question of how best to unleash the hidden potential of the country's young population in order to realize the hope for a new and different future.

The next day on campus, I found Jeevan and his friends standing by the tea stalls. When I asked Jeevan whether he was satisfied with the outcome of his initiative, he replied: 'What I am doing is not much profitable and long-term. So, I am doing all these things because I have to be involved. It is the lack of opportunity that motivates me to do something.' His friend gave Jeevan a pat on his back and affirmed: 'Without a goal in life, it ends up being a destinationless journey, and then nothing would be achieved. But we are not *ābāra* yuba.' Literally translated to English, 'ābāra yuba' means 'vagabond youth'. The Nepali word 'ābāra' is generally used to describe somebody who wanders around doing nothing. This kind of aimlessness, according to the students, was closely associated with a number of vices, including dishonour, selfishness, irresponsibility, and uselessness.

The students continued to explain to me that ābāra yuba were also those of their peers who just hung out on the campus, ready to pick up a fight. Much to everybody's amusement, Upendra, who had also participated in the cleaning campaign at the hospital, demonstrated:

They will just go like a horse! [he puts his hands next to his eyes like blinkers and mimics a furious gallop] 'We can develop the nation!

[2] In November 2011, I attended the first Surya Nepal Asha Social Entrepreneurship Award ceremony and recorded my observations and parts of the speeches by high-ranked Nepali intellectuals, industrialists, and other public figures in my research diary. For further information see https://snasea2013.wordpress.com/, accessed 12 November 2014.

We can! We do!' [said in a loud and angry tone] I don't listen to such things anymore. All we get told is to develop the nation. But how? There is no good logic. I don't just follow any person without knowing what for.

Sapana, with whom I had previously attended a workshop on HIV/AIDS and sexual health that had been organized by the youth organization she was a member of, picked up on this point and added:

The politicians call for more youth participation. They say that young people are supposed to be more involved in decision-making processes. But it's the same old fairy tales, no? The same has been said twenty years ago. And still today youth are said to be the country's change agents. But I don't know who calls himself a 'change agent'. I certainly don't.

These opinions met with the group's general approval.

More than half of the 40 students I interviewed had repeatedly participated in some kind of youth-led campaign or were an active member of a youth club at the time of my field research. It was important for these students to emphasize that the youth organizations in which they were involved were different from the campus-based student organizations. Established student organizations, they argued, maintained close ties with political parties and, therefore, only appealed to those who wanted to forge a career in the government sector. Otherwise, there was no use of getting involved in a student organization as the so-called 'student leaders' retained all the power and influence, despite being 40 years and older (see also Snellinger 2009). Those students who did not want to take a stance in party politics or were unwilling to submit to hierarchical structures, therefore, often started their own youth clubs outside existing university or state structures (see also Poudel and de Schepper 2010).

During a visit to the office of one of these youth organizations, it became evident to me that this form of joint activity provided an important site of identification, especially for those educated young Nepalis who lived and studied in their home country. The most dominant feature in the otherwise sparsely furnished room was a wall hanging made of a large straw mat of the kind traditionally used as a sleeping mattress or seat pad. For the youth organization, however, it served a different purpose. Around five large orange letters, which spelled the English word 'youth', they had written down with colourful paints whom they wanted to take part in their organization. The straw mat now listed the ages from 16 to 29 years, a number of describing words, including energetic, hard-working, creative, smart, curious, trustworthy, optimistic, and new generation, and the English pronoun 'I' (see Figure 5.2). They had made it a rule that anyone older than 29 years was no longer permitted to be a member of the organization and members could be part of the executive board only once for a period of two years.

The five members present in the office explained to me that, before they had formally established the organization three years ago, they sat together and discussed which interests they shared:

> We used to study in different colleges and we rarely had any similarities. At that time, we were nine persons of nine different kinds. But each of us was determined to do something. We all thought that we must do something living here in Nepal. In contrast to most of our peers, we did not like to compromise our dignity just to obtain a visa. All of us were like that.

One of the members grew up as the only son of an upper-middle-class family in Kathmandu and studied for a master's degree in international development at the privately run Kathmandu University. Another one was a young Gurung man, who had moved to Kathmandu from a rural area in the east of the country and was enrolled at the central department of sociology of Tribhuvan University. A third member, a young Brahmin woman, was studying for a degree in economics and had completed her schooling in Jumla, a small town in the mountainous parts of western Nepal. Hearing more about each member's family and educational background confirmed my impression that these young Nepalis identified more strongly with one another based on their shared experiences as university students in Kathmandu and their joint future vision of staying in Nepal than on the basis of traditional social markers, such as gender, ethnicity, or caste (cf. Faye 2017).

Figure 5.2   Wall-Hanging in the Office of a Youth Club in Kathmandu, January 2012
Source: Author

It was not uncommon for students to dedicate a significant share of their time and energy to youth-led initiatives. In 2011, Jeevan was actively involved in five different voluntary projects and youth organizations for which he invested around 40 hours per week. Jeevan told me that he grew up with the belief that his chances of accessing education and finding a decent job were severely limited because he was a Dalit. After he did not succeed in finding a paid job, he started to work as a volunteer: 'And then, people started to call me for meetings and asked me to join for different activities. They had no problem with me. I mean, I can talk well, I can dress well, I am educated. And it was nice to meet so many different people. That is why I decided to work in the social sector.' Jeevan had already accumulated more than five years of experience as a volunteer for non-profit organizations. He was fortunate that his older siblings, who worked as schoolteachers, earned an income which was sufficient to provide for his family. This way, he felt less pressured to assume financial responsibility and could pursue his aspiration for a career in the development sector. He explained: 'Our education system is not very practical. But you can make up for this if you are proactive yourself. But if you are not active and if you only rely on your university education, you may not necessarily get the skills that employers look for. A master's degree alone will not make you a suitable candidate.'

Similar to Jeevan, other students also strongly believed that the experiences and skills they gained through their involvement in youth-led initiatives were more valuable than the book knowledge taught at university. They argued that their roles and responsibilities within youth organizations allowed them to advance their computer and media skills, learn how to work in a team, acquire insights into the institutional structures of international organizations, become familiar with the terminology of development discourses, and build relevant social contacts. Many of the students I spoke with hoped that their experiences as members of youth organizations, in combination with their academic credentials, would help them to embark on a career in the highly competitive development sector in Nepal.

***

The conversations I had with students about their career aspirations revealed the large extent to which it mattered for these educated young Nepalis to meet others' expectations and to realize the future life paths which were commonly perceived to be desirable and auspicious. Bishal, who, in 2011, was 23 years old and studied for a master's degree in rural development on Patan Campus, put it in a nutshell by saying: 'The destination of our generation is money as well as name. Money is absolutely essential in our life. Name is also important for ijjat, meaning honour and prestige. Money and name are connected.' Other possible translations of the Nepali word 'ijjat' include 'dignity', 'respectability', and 'reputation' (Cameron 1998; Liechty 2003; Rankin 2004). While ascribed facts of birth, such as caste and gender, help define what will be judged as honourable behaviour, ijjat is largely an achieved state (Cameron 1998). It is not to be gained through a one-off performance, but instead needs to be actively earned and continuously reproduced over time. Staking claims in the social economy of ijjat, therefore, demands a steady and sufficient flow of monetary means (Rankin 2004). Economic success is consequently often a precondition for the possession of ijjat (see also Liechty 2003: 84).

Throughout the twentieth century, a university education was seen to provide a sure-fire route to social success, not least because university graduates often came to hold high-status positions in the public sector (TU 1996; see also Liechty 2003). In order to be eligible to apply for the position of a government officer, it was sufficient to hold a bachelor's degree. However, only four out of the 40 master's students I interviewed were interested in applying for a post in the public administration. In this context, Uttam, a 24-year-old Chhetri man, told me:

> I am not studying management to then end up sitting the whole day in an office doing nothing. The only thing I would have to do is this. [He stands up abruptly and takes a deep bow.] Every time an important person walks in. [laughs and adds in Nepali] *beijjat*. You know beijjat? It means the work is not honourable.

Uttam's father had been employed as a civil servant at district level during his entire working life. Uttam acknowledged that his family had greatly benefited from the father's regular salary and that he would not have been able to finance his university studies without his father's support. Nonetheless, he had no intention of following in his father's footsteps, mainly because an employment in the public sector was no longer perceived to provide a good reputation (ijjat). Rather, the opposite was the case: dishonour (beijjat). Similar to Uttam, most of his peers associated the governmental sector with obsolete structures and corrupt practices.

On one occasion, in January 2012, I was walking with Sabita, a 25-year-old Chhetri woman who was studying for a master's degree in sociology on Patan Campus, past an office building of the UN in Kathmandu—its golden emblem and waving flags were widely visible. Once we got to the entrance gate of the UN complex, Sabita slowed down and sighed: 'Don't you want to come here one day and say, "This is my office!"?' Sabita articulated a hope shared by many of her peers, especially those enrolled in graduate programmes in the social sciences and humanities. Bishal had told me before that he wanted to set up his own NGO to develop educational programmes for community radio stations in rural areas of Nepal. Uttam dearly hoped to find a job in the human resources department of an international NGO. Overall, half of the 40 students I interviewed explicitly stated that they aspired to engage in social work or some kind of development project. The non-governmental sector, they argued, offered a dynamic work environment in which educated young people, like themselves, could make use of their qualifications and youthful vigour.

Following the re-establishment of a multiparty democracy in Nepal and the reinstatement of the fundamental right to organize in the early 1990s, the nature and scale of non-governmental activities changed immensely. Under the new legislation, voluntary associations were allowed to operate freely and NGOs were actively encouraged to take charge of the delivery of public services to compensate for the state's failures (Heaton-Shrestha 2002). Available figures suggest that the number of registered international and national NGOs in Nepal increased from 1,210 in 1993 to 39,759 in 2014.[3] While the idea of contributing to the social good continued

[3] Data on the growth of the number of NGOs in Nepal was retrieved from the Social Welfare Council Nepal; see http://www.swc.org.np/ngo-ingos-charts-2070071/, accessed 15 August 2018.

to motivate people to take part in activities of non-profit organizations, development work was also seen to be a way to tap into the enormous amount of aid money flowing into the country (Faye 2017; Heaton-Shrestha and Adhikari 2011; Liechty 2003). A career in the non-governmental sector promised to offer a whole range of financial and social benefits, which were hard to find in any other segment of Nepal's labour market. As a result, an entire 'development industry' (Basnett 2012) had emerged around the work ethos of serving the country.

Still, the daily job realities of those young Nepalis involved in non-profit organizations had often little to do with the professional careers they aspired to. When I met Ranjan, a 25-year-old Brahmin man, for the first time in October 2011, he proudly presented me with his business card, according to which he was a 'member of the executive board' and the 'general secretary' of a local NGO. Ranjan had established the organization together with some friends who, like himself, had studied for a degree in rural development. With a sense of duty, he explained to me: 'As students of rural development, we need to try to uplift Nepali people who live in rural areas. This is our small effort. We hope that we will be able to uplift them after some years.'

The next time I met Ranjan on campus, he came prepared with a big folder that included mission statements, project plans, and organizational diagrams. He enthusiastically described in detail each of the initiatives outlined in the pages. Over the next couple of months, I continued to see Ranjan and his friends from the master's programme in rural development regularly around campus and, eventually, we agreed that I should visit him at his workplace before I leave Nepal. The office turned out to be a sparely furnished room on the ground floor of his uncle's house located in a middle-class residential area of the city. It was during this visit that Ranjan told me that none of the project ideas had so far been implemented. Moreover, rather than earning an income, he kept on investing not only time and effort but also his own money in the organization in the hope of establishing himself as a development expert. Due to cases such as Ranjan's, the booming NGO sector had indeed become an object of ridicule (Heaton-Shrestha 2002: 8–9). In particular, it has been criticized that the main beneficiaries of the ongoing process of 'NGO-ization' were not the poor, but the founders of the NGOs themselves (Heaton-Shrestha and Adhikari 2011; see also Jad 2007). However, even if the hope of a lucrative career often remained unfulfilled, by setting up an NGO, a younger family member could at least be provided with a respectable job as a development aid worker (see also Heaton-Shrestha 2010).

Precisely because of economic constraints, some of the students I spoke with had to depart from their initial ambitions to forge a career in the non-profit sector. For example, Karuna, who grew up in Kathmandu as the only daughter of a relatively poor upper-caste family, had decided to study sociology in the hope of finding a job with a development agency. However, when I met Karuna in December 2011, she had just started to work for a private business in the media sector alongside her university studies. Her boyfriend, who was employed by the same company, had helped her secure the job. Her parents, who worked as service staff in a hotel in Kathmandu, earned barely enough to cover the family's living expenses. So, she was glad to be able to contribute to her family's income. At the same time, Karuna was afraid that she may not keep the job in the long run since she had not been trained in a relevant subject and, therefore, struggled to fulfil the job requirements. When I asked her whether she would consider changing her job again in order to do something more in line with her educational qualifications and her personal interests, she replied somewhat hesitantly:

There are these programmes for youth on issues such as women's empowerment, child labour or so. I've seen it on the news. But I think these programmes that you see on television are only for those associated with the UN, or the government, or indigenous or marginalized people. Of course, I would also like to take part in those programmes. But I don't think that I'm eligible to participate and I wouldn't know how to go there. There is no channel for general people like us.

Following the conversation with Karuna, I was interested to find out whether, and, if so, how, young educated Nepalis managed to secure a position with an international donor agency. I contacted Sujit, whom I had met one time on campus during an induction programme for newly admitted students. At this stage, Sujit had been living in Kathmandu for three months only. He had moved to the capital city after being offered a job at the office of an international donor agency, where he was earning an above-average income.

When we met again, I learned that Sujit identified himself as a Dalit and that he had grown up in a village located at the western border of Nepal, one of the most neglected regions in terms of infrastructural development. From there, it took about half a day by foot and by bus to reach Mahendranagar, the district headquarters, which was renamed Bheemdatt in 2008. Sujit's parents were subsistence farmers and were still living in the village. His older brother had got married at the age of 14 and, subsequently, left school in grade 8 in order to take up a job in a trading company in Mahendranagar. Though Sujit too started to engage in paid labour at the age of 16, he had continued to attend secondary school. One of his teachers had recommended him to volunteer for a small community-building project. The organizers of the development project took notice of Sujit because he was one of the few people in the village with good literacy and numeracy skills. They offered him work for a library project in Mahendranagar. The job only earned him a few hundred rupees but gave Sujit the opportunity to acquire some English-language skills and learn how to use a computer. Equipped with these competencies, Sujit was hired by different NGOs to work for development initiatives at district level in the following years: 'During these past 10 years, I saw so many things in social and development sector. Main thing is I got in contact with government bodies, people in the village administration, different NGOs, donor agencies, women committees, and so on.' Apart from building a network with various actors involved in planned development, Sujit also got a chance to move to the city of Dhangadhi for work purposes. There, he enrolled as an undergraduate student at the local college. Once he completed his bachelor's degree, he applied for a vacancy published by his current employer and was selected. After working for one-and-a-half years at the regional office of the international NGO, he was offered a post in the Kathmandu office.

Over the course of my conversation with Sujit, it became evident that his educational and occupational trajectories were closely inter-linked in such a way that his achievements in school and at work had only been possible in combination. Without a paid job, Sujit would not have been able to finance his studies or access institutions of higher education, which existed exclusively in the urban centres of Nepal. Without completing his schooling and obtaining a university degree, he would have stood a poor chance of securing a job in the highly competitive development sector. It had often been difficult for him to juggle these competing priorities. Two times, he was unable to take the exams at the end of the academic year because he was involved in development projects located in remote parts of the Far-Western Region. For this reason, he took five instead of three years to complete the undergraduate programme. Likewise, Sujit was mostly absent from the campus during my research stay in Kathmandu since he frequently had to travel to his home region for work purposes. I asked Sujit whether he intended to stay in Kathmandu in the future, to which he replied:

> No, I want to go back to the Far West. That's good for me. It is my birthplace and I started my career in the development sector from there. I know much more about there than I do about here. I know what the issues are in the Far West and how to solve them.... One of my colleagues studied in the Netherlands about human rights. He is always telling me about the style of teaching and education system there. But my mind is not set to go abroad. My priority is to study here and work here in Nepal, work for my Far West.

***

The majority of the young Nepalis featuring in this book genuinely strove to live up to familial and social expectations. To this end, dominant discourses about the role of educated youth in Nepali society served as important points of reference and influenced their moral conceptions. At the same time, they were acutely aware of the gap that existed between the futures they were encouraged to aspire to and the opportunities available to them. In the highly competitive urban labour market, a university education per se no longer provided an entrance ticket to professional employment. Yet, most of the students of Patan Campus did not have the financial backing which would have allowed them to engage in strategic forms of 'waiting' to prolong their education until an adequate employment became available (cf. Jeffrey 2010b; Liechty 2003). 'Spatial fixes' (Mains 2012) to immediate problems of unemployment and political insecurity in the form of international migration were likewise not an option readily available to most of the young Nepalis I met in Kathmandu. Still, I found that the students of Patan Campus, by and large, managed to maintain a sense of hope and a positive outlook regarding their own future lives.

In line with Johnson-Hanks's (2002) argument, I therefore hold that variations in young people's practices and future orientations should not be exclusively viewed with concern over their seeming inability to realize socially valued future pathways. Rather, I argue that it is important to appreciate the variety of young people's practices as it reveals a lot about the ways in which young people can gain recognition as respectable members of society. An analysis of students' attempts to map out potential future pathways in Nepal makes evident that these young people evaluated their life chances on the basis of their own lived experiences and in relation to their socio-spatial identities. I contend that such self-conscious reflections opened up opportunities for more critical engagements with dominant and often normative representations of youth.

Even though the students I spoke with, by and large, expressed a strong intention to live up to the ideal of an educated person and related familial expectations, a sense of apprehension and disillusion threaded through our conversations about what it meant to be part of Nepal's educated youth. In the eyes of many people in Kathmandu, going abroad to study in a Western country was the silver bullet for the many difficulties Nepal's younger generation was facing. Although such prevalent perceptions put a lot of pressure on young Nepalis studying in Kathmandu, staying in Nepal still represented more than just a second-best alternative for some of them. In response, these young people sought to identify themselves as the country's educated youth that took responsibility for local communities and cared for the future of their home country.

Related to this, it was greatly important for the young Nepalis I spoke with to distinguish themselves from the pervasive image of the educated unemployed who seemed to lack any purpose or direction in life. For this reason, many of them engaged in often time-consuming initiatives on a voluntary basis. Having the capacity to 'do something' constituted an important source of self-worth for these young Nepalis, not least because these grassroots-level organizations brought together young people of both genders and from different caste/ethnic and class backgrounds. Through their involvements in youth-led initiatives, they also acquired valuable insights into the local community and established personal networks which could prove useful in the modern job market. This kind of knowledge, in combination with academic credentials, they felt, could potentially help them to embark on a career in the highly competitive development sector. In particular, young people who belonged to historically marginalized social groups were often able to capitalize on their achievements. In some cases, educated young Nepalis consequently felt that they were more capable of fulfilling their social obligations and contributing to the social good if they remained relatively settled in their familiar environment.

Although such perceptions and related spatial practices deviated from pervasive and often normative discourses about young people's potential futures, I argue that it would be inaccurate to describe them as forms of resistance. It was not the intention of these young people to defy social norms and challenge dominated future visions according to which the educated youth was expected to realize the political, economic, and social future ideals which so far remained unaccomplished. Rather, these young people tried to make better sense of such widespread encouragements to achieve in the light of their own lived experiences, and they did so by appropriating dominant educational and occupational strategies. I deliberately use the term 'appropriation' as it best describes the various ways in which the research participants used the resources available to them by virtue of their socio-spatial identities and, in so doing, were capable of negotiating the multitude of competing social influences that shaped their young lives (see also Rockwell 1996).

In addition, it is necessary to emphasize that such appropriations were not the result of a 'cooling-out' process, as described by Clark (1960). The students did not simply accept their positions within the socio-spatial hierarchy in the face of persisting inequalities and constraints; quite the contrary. I found that young people's small efforts of 'doing good' helped them to grow in confidence and self-respect. In line with Kraftl (2008), I argue that small steps and relatively modest coping mechanisms often provide impulses of hopefulness, which in turn may encourage young people to start exploring different options in their own ways. My analysis of young people's time–space strategies, therefore, demonstrates that young people's agency may reside in the multiple ways in which they are able to account for competing social influences and anticipate the potential consequences of their own behaviour. In so doing, young people can foster social relationships, ensure that others support them, and hence, also gain the respect of other members of the society. However, precisely because such critical engagements are far more modest than may be expected, they have so far been overlooked in the public debate.

6

Conclusions

The stories, ideas, and sentiments shared by young Nepalis attest to the complexity of young people's attempts to identify potential pathways to construct a prosperous future life. Neither the life experiences of previous generations nor modernist discourses of youth as a crucial site for a new and different future provide reliable points of reference for young Nepalis in the light of the realities of present-day life in Kathmandu. Previously well-established life trajectories specific to people's gender and caste/ethnicity have become more complicated as young people's life chances appear to depend increasingly on their own capacity to take advantage of newly emerging educational and occupational opportunities. The large majority of young people, however, do not smoothly progress through the formal education system and into the labour market; instead, they divert from the dominant and, by and large, Western-inspired models of how the life course should unfold.

This trend towards diversification of young people's life paths has been observed in similar ways in the context of young people's lives in various parts of the world. Cynthia Lloyd's (2005) survey of young people in Asia, Africa, and Latin America shows that processes of globalization and urbanization have significantly transformed the experience of youth and ushered in new forms of social reproduction. In this context, Lloyd (2005: 1) emphasizes that 'traditional

expectations regarding future employment prospects and life experiences are no longer valid.' This greater degree of variability and
uncertainty has been interpreted by some social scientists as a sign
of young people's growing inability to attain socially valued forms
of adulthood, raising concerns over potentially adverse social effects
of this apparent 'crisis' of youth (Weiss 2004: 14–16; see also Dore
1976; Honwana and de Boeck 2005; Sommers 2012).

It is possible to draw parallels between these studies of youth
in other countries in the Global South and the situation of young
people in Nepal. Processes of economic liberalization and the mobi-
lization around formal education in Nepal have played out in highly
divergent ways. As a result, it has become increasingly difficult for
young Nepalis to capitalize on their educational attainments and
embark on promising career paths commonly associated with the
tertiarization of the economy. Similar to most of their peers in other
parts of the world, young people in Nepal therefore see themselves
confronted with the challenge of aligning heightened aspirations for
social ascent and a financially secure future with the often incompatible realities of their daily lives. Other researchers have linked
these developments to the emergence of youth (yuba) as a new social
category in Nepali society, arguing that youth, on the one hand,
represents a crucial site for a new and different future and, on the
other hand, is indicative of a growing surplus of adults-in-waiting
(Liechty 2003; Snellinger 2009, 2013).

By contrast, my own research with young people in Kathmandu
problematizes such pervasive depictions of youth as the makers
or breakers of future society. It does so by synthesizing different
strands of research on youth, aspiration, and mobility. This analytical approach has allowed me to foreground how young people
themselves think about their future prospects and why young people
may reassess, change, or even drop existing future orientations as
they get exposed to new ideas and influences over time and across
space. In this way, I have developed a fuller understanding of the
varied nature of young people's agency. In addition, I have critically
engaged with wider debates about the need to produce 'aspirational
citizens' and about the relationship between spatial (im)mobility and
social ascent. In the remainder of this final chapter, I outline these
main contributions to the existing literature on youth, aspiration,

and mobility in more detail and point out potential directions for future research.

Youth Agency as an Expression of Sociality and Reflexivity

Researchers across the social sciences now broadly agree that young people should not be treated as adults in the making, but as competent social actors in their own right (for example, Bucholtz 2002; Hall and Jefferson 1975; Skelton and Valentine 1997). However, precisely because researchers working with young people have long been concerned with demonstrating that young people are actively involved in the making of their social spaces, extant research chiefly documents instances in which young people break with the established social order and advertise their own individuality (see Chapter 1). As a result, a large share of the contributions made to youth studies and related sub-disciplines, such as children's geographies, tend to give the misleading impression that youth agency is synonymous with resistance and independent selfhood. However, in order to avoid contributing to the reproduction of stereotypical ideas attached to the category of youth, we have to move beyond primarily searching for evidence to underpin the claim that young people have agency. Rather, we need to explore what types of agency do young people demonstrate (see also Ahearn 2001b; Collins et al. 2013; Durham 2008).

In this book, I have shed more light on young people's capacity to act by calling attention to a group of young people who have so far been systematically neglected in public and scholarly debates about youth. The young Nepalis I worked with were not involved in any spectacular forms of youth activism. Rather, they were committed to studying well and working hard in order to improve their own and their families' situation. Other youth researchers commonly use terms such as 'ordinary' or 'conformist' to refer to young people who are not part of a distinct youth subculture and for whom school and work are more significant than fashion trends and party politics (for example, Jenkins 1983; Woodman 2013; Yoon 2006). Based on my own research, however, I argue that the implied dichotomy between 'conformist' and 'deviant' youth oversimplifies the ways in which young people may negotiate the multitude of social influences that shape their lives.

This is an important point to make, not only within the context of the debate about young people's role in the wider society but also with respect to the relevant literature on the concept of agency. There has been a general tendency to romanticize the agency of subordinate groups—be it young people, women, the indigenous, or the poor (for example, Durham 2008; Mahmood 2005; Scott 1986). This is because many studies of human agency 'are ultimately more concerned with finding resistors and explaining resistance than with examining power', as Lila Abu-Lughod (1990: 41) aptly explains. Drawing from ethnographic research with Bedouin tribes in Egypt, Abu-Lughod shows that women, on the one hand, did not simply accept the patriarchal system, but often voiced their disagreement in an indirect and shrewd manner. On the other hand, the same young women tended to readily consent to newly emerging systems of dominance in the form of religious education because of its association with a modern lifestyle. As a result, wider structures of male dominance were often reinforced or, at least, remained unchallenged.

In a similar vein, I found that the young Nepalis I spoke with tried to set themselves apart from their parents and less educated peers in order to nurture their own social status as an educated and successful person. To the extent that these young people advanced to higher levels of education, engaged in jobs outside traditional sectors, and were more receptive to new technologies and global migration trends than the parental generation, they indeed seemed to move towards a new and different future. At the same time, it became evident in our conversations that, without the support of their parents, siblings, and friends, most of the research participants would have been unlikely to benefit from the newly emergent educational and occupational opportunities in the first place. Consequently, it is difficult to categorize young people's behaviour using the dichotomy of resistance versus compliance. Based on an in-depth analysis of the ways in which young people relate to a range of other social actors, I have been able to clearly show that elements of both resistance and compliance are present in most social interactions, with the result that their specific outcomes for wider society are often hard to predict.

These empirical findings also show that it may not even be in the interest of young people to break from their familiar environment and demonstrate a greater degree of independence. This is partly because close ties with the family and the home community generally serve as an important security network through which young people are able to access financial support as well as valuable social contacts. For exactly this reason, the pursuit of an urban lifestyle or an international education often constituted a joint family project, rather than a decision that young Nepalis made on their own. Also, in the case of those young people whose families lacked sufficient economic and social resources to provide much support to the off-spring, it was still important for young people to 'do something' for their communities and, more generally, the home country.

This strong sense of social responsibility expressed by all of the research participants needs to be understood within the context of Nepal's ijjat economy. Young people in Nepal were acutely aware that their social standing was judged not solely with respect to their position within social hierarchies of gender, class, and caste/ethnicity, but also based on their contributions towards the wider community (Chapters 4 and 5). With the emergence of a modern education system in Nepal, these culturally embedded values have become even further manifested in the minds of Nepal's younger generation. National and international policymakers alike continue to promote the idea that it is the responsibility of educated youth to contribute to the social good and work for the development of the country. The vision of youth activism emerging from young Nepalis' own reflections and public discourses differs significantly from prevalent conceptualizations of youth agency as active efforts to become more independent from cultural or social constructions. Instead, it suggests that young people in Nepal grow in power as they learn to fulfil social obligations and foster stronger relationships with other people. In line with past studies of young people's agency in Africa (Durham 2008), Latin America (Punch 2002), and Asia (Dyson 2014), I, therefore, argue that there is a need to free the concept of agency from its narrow association with resistance and autonomous selfhood.

My work with young people in Nepal, however, differs from these ethnographic accounts in some important respects. While these studies of young people's agency place the focus of analysis on young people's practices as they are observed in the present,

I have specifically emphasized young people's narratives about the future. In this respect, it has proven useful to build on Johnson-Hanks's (2002) theory of vital conjunctures in order to untangle critical decision-making situations where the choices young people make, or that others make on their behalf, are likely to have an impact on their life chances in the long term. This analytical focus on certain vital conjunctures that young people experience over the course of their educational and occupational careers has allowed me to elucidate how these young people developed certain ideas about their own future in relation to the social influences and structuring forces that shape their lives. In particular, I have shown that a multitude of structuring forces and social pressures—parents, peers, political leaders, private entrepreneurs, the media—bear down hard on educated young people as these actors try to project their own future visions onto the lives of the younger generation. However, my empirical findings also illustrate well that young people are capable of negotiating such critical situations during which potential futures are under debate in various ways. By framing their educational and occupational experiences as vital conjunctures, I have been able to anticipate this curious combination of structures pressing down hard but, simultaneously, agency being expressed on the part of the young people involved. Thus, I could capture more unexpected and perhaps counter-intuitive variations in young people's perceptions and experiences and, in turn, develop a fuller understanding of the varied nature of young people's agency.

At the same time, I contend that the concept of vital conjunctures needs further development in order to better account for how young people may rethink existing future orientations as they get exposed to new ideas and influences over time and across space. More than Johnson-Hanks (2002) did in her study of young women in Cameroon, it is necessary to attend to the politics involved in the formation of young people's future orientations. By looking more closely at the exact content and nature of the aspirations of educated young Nepalis, I have uncovered the paradoxical nature of aspirations, which can suggest limitations as much as goals. In addition, Johnson-Hanks's strong emphasis on the idea that changes in young people's lives occur across multiple temporalities downplays the significance of different forms of spatial mobility for their developing identities and, in relation to this, their future orientations. In order to supplement Johnson-Hanks's theoretical contribution, I have traced young people's perceptions and practices in a variety of socio-spatial settings. These are important contributions that this book makes to the wider debates in and beyond human geography. I, therefore, discuss these two points in more detail with reference to the concepts of aspiration and mobility.

The Potential and the Limitations of Politics of Aspiration Building

Visions of a new and different future are commonly fed by large-scale structural changes as well as developmental and political agendas for economic growth and social equity. Such rhetoric of hope and opportunity are often directed at young people as they are seen to still have an entire life to build (for example, Davidson 2011; Kraftl 2008; Meinert 2009; Raco 2009). In the case of Nepal, raised expectations for the younger generation can be specifically linked to the establishment of a mass education system during the second half of twentieth century (Skinner and Holland 1996; Valentin 2005). The promises associated with these new educational opportunities have, for the most part, not been fulfilled. Even so, I found that hopes for economic progress and social advancement are still kept alive by influential public figures in Nepal, namely, political leaders and international donors, who try to promote micro-level forms of entrepreneurship, or private agents, who seek to sell the dream of studying and living in one of the countries perceived to be at the very centre of the global knowledge system. Consequently, visions of youth as 'pioneers of economic, social, political, and culture transformation' (MoYS 2010) are not only manifested in the National Youth Policy, 2010, but are also widely circulated through marketing campaigns, civic development programmes, and mass media in Nepal.

In this respect, I concur with Appadurai's (2004: 61) assertion that it is important to 'bring the future back in' in order to gain a better understanding of how individuals navigate their social spaces. What people believe might be possible in the future serves as a strong reference point for their decisions and actions in the present, even though the future remains inherently uncertain. This point

forcefully emerges from my analysis of the motivations and aspirations behind the choices young Nepalis make with regard to their
educational careers (Chapter 3). Academic credentials have come
to represent a valuable cultural resource as they promise to enable
the younger generation to gain social distinction and improve their
own and their families' economic situation. Families from across
the social strata, therefore, are willing to spend a large share of the
household's budget for their children's education. As a result, a
growing number of young Nepalis, including those who come from
social groups previously not represented at university, have been
able to follow educational trajectories that bear no comparison with
the much more basic levels of education attained by the parental
generation. In view of this generational disjuncture, Debra Skinner
and Dorothy Holland (1996: 291) have argued that educated young
Nepalis 'were creating new identities and self-understandings that
resisted older forms of privilege'. While I agree that educational success was an important source of self-worth for the young Nepalis I
spoke with, I contest that these young people were resisting or even
dismissing established norms and values. Rather, I found that young
people's aspirations for a future life that would be different from that
of their parents or less educated peers merely reflected widespread
social expectations for educated youth. Based on these empirical
findings, I hold that a future-oriented approach to young people's
agency opens up new perspectives as it calls attention to collective
future visions which inform the choices individuals make.

At the same time, my study shows that such politics of aspiration
building are often only of limited success. In part, this is because
socially instilled aspirations tend to reproduce existing social
inequalities. There are some parallels here with recent research on
the politics involved in the formation of young people's aspirations.
Similar to studies conducted with young women in India (Donner
2005; Rao 2010), it became apparent in the conversations I had
with young Nepali women that they strove to attain higher levels
of education mainly because they wanted to conform to the image
of a modern, educated woman in the hope of entering a favourable
marriage arrangement. In comparison, young men sought to keep
pace with the educational race in order to live up to established
notions of respectable masculinity, which meant that they sought

to take financial and social responsibility for their families and the wider community. Because of these established gender roles, young men also felt pressured to migrate abroad, while young women felt discouraged to even obtain more information about international degree programmes (Chapters 3 and 5).

In this context, I furthermore found that the social practices of Kathmandu's upper-middle class and the established elite served as important points of reference for aspirational young people, who attempted to map out potential ways of constructing a prosperous future life. A private education, a foreign degree obtained in a Western anglophone country, and a job in the development industry were seen to be highly desirable life achievements, not least because they were closely associated with the urban propertied classes. In this respect, my findings also lend support to studies conducted in countries in the Global North, which likewise reveal that efforts to produce 'active, responsible, educational citizens' tend to reassert middle-class hegemony (Reay 2008; see also Davidson 2011; Holloway and Pimlott-Wilson 2011; Raco 2009).

Moreover, the idea that the production of 'aspirational citizens' will lead to enhanced opportunities for social ascent ignores that young people's difficulties to become upwardly mobile cannot exclusively, and sometimes not even primarily, be attributed to low aspirations. Similar to other researchers working in Nepal (Liechty 2003; Valentin 2005) and, more generally, in countries in the Global South (Jeffrey 2010b; Mains 2012; Meinert 2009), my observations imply that encouragements given to young people to capitalize on their educational attainments tend to take little account of the wider social, political, and economic circumstances that shape young people's lives. At times of lingering political and economic crises in particular, discourses of hope and opportunity may consequently raise young people's anxieties regarding the future, rather than provide a source of inspiration. This is because young people's future orientations are never entirely or exclusively framed by the future visions that other social actors try to project onto them. So, on the one hand, first-generation university students in Nepal seemed to embody the widespread hope that newly emergent educational and occupational opportunities also opened up possibilities for a greater degree of social equality. On the other hand, these young people had to realize that conventional tokens of success, such as a university degree or urban life, no longer fulfilled the promises they once held, as more privileged social groups sought out educational pathways for their offspring outside the state system or even outside the country. With reference to similar situations in the case of young people in African countries, other researchers have expressed concerns over the imminent risk of social unrest and political instability, should the link between young people's hope for a better future and its fulfilment be cut (Mains 2012; Sommers 2012; Vigh 2006).

My analysis, however, suggests that young people were generally capable of negotiating such pressured situations in an effective manner. In our conversations, it became apparent that young Nepalis seriously thought about what motivated them, which resources they could draw from, and how certain steps might help them to achieve their future objectives. At the same time, these young people were self-consciously aware of the gap that existed between the future they felt encouraged to aspire to and the realities of present-day life in Kathmandu. Such reflections opened up opportunities for more critical engagements with dominant and universalizing discourses on the role of educated youth in society. In line with Kraftl's (2008) work on hope and childhood, I hold that it is highly instructive in this context to account for both dominant discourses on the role of youth in wider society and young people's own articulations of hope. More specifically, I argue that particular attention needs to be paid to the small and often unexpected steps that enable young people to maintain a sense of hope and a positive outlook regarding their own future lives. This is because I found that such modest forms of hoping may constitute valid coping strategies that allow young people to make better sense of the disconnect between dominant future visions and the realities of their everyday lives.

Consequently, the value of a future-oriented approach to young people's agency is that it allows grasping how young people actively plan and plot their actions not only based on lived experiences but also in anticipation of the opportunities and constraints that may present themselves in the future. My findings illustrate well that young people negotiate important decision-making situations during which potential futures are under debate by drawing on various points of reference, whether these are in the now and here or imagined as yet to come. As a result of such self-conscious reflections, young people's aspirations are not simply 'cooled out'. Through modest appropriations of dominant educational and occupational strategies, young people are instead able to sustain a sense of hope and agency in the present, without completely abandoning more ambitious plans for the future. I, therefore, argue that educated young people in Kathmandu have been able to move towards a hopeful future along multi-lane routes.

In view of these findings, I furthermore contend that Appadurai's (2004) conceptualization of the capacity to aspire requires some modification. My findings clearly show that it is not sufficient to strengthen young people's capacity to envision promising educational and occupational pathways in order to enable them to improve their lives. An analysis of young people's life chances instead needs to verify to what extent such heightened aspirations tally with the economic and social opportunities available to young people. By attending to how young people's future orientations relate them to other social actors, I have been able to develop a better understanding of young people's capacity to act upon the world reflexively, yet without neglecting the limits to young people's agency in the form of social hierarchies and structural constraints.

Navigating an Interconnected World

Much of the active debate about the intensification of human mobility tends to imply that it is possible to distinguish between movers and non-movers (for example, Cohen and Sirkeci 2011: 87–96; Hammer and Tamas 1997). Such a sharp distinction, however, starts to become blurred once various forms of mobility and the ways in which they are connected to each other and across different scales are taken into consideration (Adey 2010; Cresswell 2010, 2011). The young Nepalis featuring in this study had no personal experience of cross-border travels and, hence, seemed to be relatively immobile in comparison with the growing number of international migrants, who have been given most attention in the scholarship on migration and mobilities (see also Fortier 2014). However, it emerges from my fieldwork that the young people I met in Kathmandu were directly affected by the trend towards out-migration from Nepal.

They were constantly exposed to images of foreign countries and stories of diasporic Nepalis through educational marketing, mass media, online interactions, and, in a few cases, kinship ties. Such encounters formed an integral part of young people's lives in Kathmandu, not least because they had to criss-cross the city on a daily basis in order to attend to their studies at university as well as their jobs in offices and schools located in different parts of the city. By applying a more comprehensive perspective to young people's spatial practices as promoted within the 'new mobilities paradigm', I have identified various ways in which educated young people in Kathmandu were actively engaged in different forms of spatial mobility and immobility. In so doing, I offer an account of young people's mobility practices and related social effects which complicates dualistic classifications of youth and, more generally, adds to our understanding of the relationship between mobility and immobility.

Several scholars involved in research on mobility topics have critically noted that, in contemporary social thought, spatial mobility is commonly associated with a greater potential for liberation and social ascent, whereas spatial immobility has increasingly acquired the connotation of backwardness, failure, and being left behind (for example, Adey et al. 2014; Cresswell 2006; Morley 2000). The same tendencies can be observed in the case of Nepali society. The ways in which specific places are promoted as being more developed and sophisticated reinvigorate fantasies and desires that drive people to move to the city, or further afield, in search of presumably better lives elsewhere. My empirical findings suggest that dominant future strategies for social advancements were largely 'anti-local', in the sense that places located beyond the confines of young people's familiar environment were generally perceived to be more advanced and sophisticated. To some extent, this spatial connotation of opportunity and prosperity is closely bound up with the culturally embedded concept of 'para', which implies that it is necessary for people to move beyond the regular boundaries of home in order to take advantage of better opportunities elsewhere (Chapter 2). As a result of the changes in the educational and economic landscape of Nepal, a hierarchy of desirable destinations for education has emerged, with more distant places being ranked the highest. Young people who grew up in parts of the country located

outside the Kathmandu Valley, therefore, commonly aspired to relocate to the capital city; and those who were living in the capital city for
a longer period aspired to migrate abroad. Thus, it can be concluded
that young people's future orientations were significantly shaped
by their socio-spatial origins, with the result that rural youth perceived themselves as being less ambitious and progressive than
their urban peers. For similar reasons, many of the young people I
spoke with also felt anxious about the fact they were only indirectly
connected with places outside Nepal's borders (Chapter 3). Such
sentiments of lagging behind simply because people feel rooted in
their home communities are indicative of the power of modernist
and developmental discourses and the imagined geographies they
produce to locate people on the margins (see also Massey 1993).

Despite such prevalent sentiments, I found that the relationship between young people's mobility practices and their chances
of social ascent is much more complex than dominant discourses
suggest. In this respect, my work contributes to a strand of research
which shows that people's movements are structured by gender,
class, and ethnicity and that migration, in turn, affects social relations and people's life chances. With reference to research into
rural-to-urban labour migration in countries in Asia and Africa,
Arjan de Haan and Ben Rogaly (2002: 6) aptly summarize this
point as they write: 'the specific way in which migration is arranged
and what it means to particular people is bound up with social
identities. Who the migrant thinks she or he is affects the type
of migration.' In line with this argument, I have discussed that
education-related mobility was seen to be a way for young Nepalis
to distinguish themselves from their less privileged peers, who were
said to carry out manual work back in the village or low-prestige
jobs in countries in the Gulf region and Southeast Asia. More than
students' individual performance at university, education-related
mobilities—be it the daily commute to campus or the move to
the capital city to continue to higher levels of education—were a
source of self-worth. I, however, have also shown that such prevalent associations between young people's identities and their spatial
practices sometimes worked out in reverse. For example, some
young men, unlike most young women, avoided going to campus
regularly because they were afraid of being related to campus-based

and predominately male student politics, as such an association would have posed a risk to the social reputation these young men sought to maintain (Chapter 4). My empirical findings illustrate well that the social implications of people's spatial mobilities need to be explored in relation to both people's self-perceptions and the socio-spatial identities that are delivered back to them from others.

A further contribution this study makes to the ongoing debate about enhanced levels of human mobility and potential social implications relates to the question of why some people remain relatively immobile. The insights I gained into young people's time–space strategies suggest that the decision to stay rooted in place is not necessarily only a back-up plan, but may as well be a preferred option. Similar to Fischer and Malmberg (2001), I found that young people were sometimes able to utilize and maximize their 'location-specific insider advantages'. The knowledge and experiences that some young Nepalis acquired locally, and specifically at the village level, significantly gained in value the moment these insights opened up opportunities to secure one of the highly sought-after jobs with an international development organization (Chapter 5). However, it also became evident in the conversations I had with young Nepalis that the decision against leaving behind their homes was not purely a rational choice made in view of the opportunity costs involved in relocating to an unfamiliar place. Rather, it was also a matter of emotional and social connectedness. Despite all the difficulties of present-day life in Nepal, I found that young Nepalis expressed a profound sense of responsibility for their families and, more generally, for the future of their home country. Such insights into young people's relationship with home (ghar) put into perspective widespread concerns regarding the much-lamented 'brain drain' and the potential costs for Nepali society.

This study then confirms and supplements some of the ideas central to the 'new mobilities paradigm'. By calling attention to a group of young people who have so far remained less visible in mobilities research, I have unpacked the complex relationship between mobility and immobility in some interesting ways. On the one hand, I have demonstrated that these seemingly sedentary youth were actively engaged in a number of different forms of mobility and, in fact, were no less affected by the great degree of global connectivity than their migrant peers. More importantly perhaps, I have shown that young people's decision to remain relatively rooted in place cannot be entirely explained by unequal power relations due to which the potential for mobility is unevenly distributed within and across societies (Massey 1993). Rather, I want to place an emphasis on the cases of those young people who were able to accumulate relevant cultural and social resources precisely because they were relatively entrenched in their home communities (Chapter 5). Based on this evidence, I argue that forms of spatial immobility may help young people to navigate an increasingly interconnected world in an effective manner and to make their futures.

Epilogue

As this book goes to press,

Shreya is working as a market research specialist for a large cooperation and lives with her husband in Kathmandu.

Dipendra is working as a senior officer for an international NGO and lives with his wife and their 5-year-old son in Kathmandu.

Deepa is a much-read journalist and writer and lives with her husband in Kathmandu.

Namita lives with her husband and their 9-month-old son in Kathmandu.

Ameena is working as a sales manager for an Indian consumer goods company and lives with her husband and their 3-year-old son in Kathmandu.

Tulasi is the principal of a private English-medium school in his hometown in Morang district, where he lives with his wife and parents.

Nischal is working in the hospitality sector and lives with his wife in Kathmandu.

Anandi is teaching at a private school and lives with her husband in Kathmandu.

Sumita lives with her husband and their 2-year-old daughter in Australia.

Rohan is working for an international NGO in close collaboration with the Ministry of Health and Population and lives with his wife and their 4-year-old daughter in Kathmandu.

Narendra is working as a Kathmandu-based research consultant for a number of international organizations and Anglo-Saxon universities.

Jeevan is working for an embassy in Kathmandu.

Sapana lives in Dhangadhi, her husband's hometown, together with her husband, their 4-year-old daughter and their 3-month-old son.

Upendra is working for a large manufacturing company and lives with his fiancée in Kathmandu.

Bishal is working as a freelance journalist and lives with his wife and parents in Kathmandu.

Sabita is working as a gender specialist for an international NGO in Kathmandu.

Ranjan is working as a project coordinator for a local NGO in Kathmandu.

Karuna is working as head of marketing for a media company and lives with her husband and their 1-year-old daughter in Kathmandu.

Sujit is working as a senior officer for an international NGO and lives with his wife and their 3-year-old son in Kathmandu.

I was unable to trace the pathways that Chitra, Sadhika, Dharana, Roshni, and Uttam have taken since 2012. However, I know that most of the other people who participated in my research project but are not explicitly mentioned in this book are still living and working in Kathmandu. Many have settled down with their partners and have become proud parents themselves. Apart from Sumita, two male research participants have moved abroad. They are presently studying at universities in Norway and Australia. I am not aware if others have continued their formal education beyond their studies at master's level on Patan Campus.

It is a joy for me to know that each one of them has made his/her future—maybe not in exactly the way they aspired to, but still in a way that appears to make them happy. Yet, it does not take away the sadness I felt when I learn about Dhirendra's death. He was killed in an accident, leaving behind his wife and their 3-year-old daughter.

Bibliography

Abu-Lughod, Lila. 1990. 'The Romance of Resistance: Tracing Transformations of Power through Bedouin Women'. *American Ethnologist* 17(1): 41–55.

Adams, Paul C. and Rina Ghose. 2003. 'India.Com: The Construction of a Space Between'. *Progress in Human Geography* 27(4): 414–37.

Adey, Peter. 2010. *Mobility*. London: Routledge.

Adey, Peter, David Bissell, Kevin Hannam, Peter Merriman, and Mimi Sheller. 2014. 'Introduction'. In P. Adey, D. Bissell, K. Hannam, P. Merriman, and M. Sheller (eds), *The Routledge Handbook of Mobilities*, pp. 1–20. London: Taylor and Francis.

Adhikari, Jagannath. 2012. 'Foreign Labour Migration and "Remittanomics"'. In *Nepal Migration Year Book 2011*, pp. 16–27. Kathmandu: Nepal Institute of Development Studies and National Centre of Competence in Research.

Adhikari, Radha. 2010. 'The "Dream-Trap": Brokering, "Study Abroad" and Nurse Migration from Nepal to the UK'. *European Bulletin of Himalayan Research* 35–6: 122–38.

Aditya, Anand, Bishnu Raj Upreti, and Poorna Kanta Adhikary. 2006. *Countries in Conflict and Processing of Peace: Lessons for Nepal*. Kathmandu: Friends for Peace.

Ahearn, Laura M. 2001a. *Invitations to Love: Literacy, Love Letters, and Social Change in Nepal*. Ann Arbor, MI: University of Michigan Press.

———. 2001b. 'Language and Agency'. *Annual Review of Anthropology* 30(1): 109–37.

Altbach, Philip G. 1989. 'The New Internationalism: Foreign Students and Scholars'. *Studies in Higher Education* 14(2): 125–36.

Altbach, Philip G. and Jane Knight. 2007. 'The Internationalization of Higher Education: Motivations and Realities'. *Journal of Studies in International Education* 11(3–4): 290–305.

Appadurai, Arjun. 2004. 'The Capacity to Aspire: Culture and the Terms of Recognition'. In V. Rao and M. Walton (eds), *Cultural and Public Action*, pp. 59–84. Stanford: Stanford University Press.

Arnett, Jeffrey J. 2000. 'Emerging Adulthood'. *American Psychologist* 55(5): 469–80.

Arnold, David and Stuart H. Blackburn. 2004. *Telling Lives in India: Biography, Autobiography, and Life History*. Delhi: Permanent Black.

Arnøy, Joakim. 2012. 'Forced Migration to, from, and within Nepal'. In *Nepal Migration Year Book 2011*, pp. 39–50. Kathmandu: Nepal Institute of Development Studies and National Centre of Competence in Research.

Baas, Michiel. 2007. 'The Language of Migration: The Education Industry versus the Migration Industry'. *People and Place* 15(2): 49–60.

Ball, Stephen J., Sheila Macrae, and Meg Maguire. 2000. *Choice, Pathways and Transitions Post-16: New Youth, New Economics in the Global City*. London: Routledge.

Barker, John, Peter Kraftl, John Horton, and Faith Tucker. 2009. 'The Road Less Travelled—New Directions in Children's and Young People's Mobility'. *Mobilities* 4(1): 1–10.

Beech, Suzanne E. 2015. 'International Student Mobility: The Role of Social Networks'. *Social & Cultural Geography* 16(3): 332–350.

Bennett, Lynn. 1983. *Dangerous Wives and Sacred Sisters: Social and Symbolic Roles of High-Caste Women in Nepal*. New York: Columbia University Press.

Bhatta, Pramod, Lila Adhikari, Manu Thada, and Ramesh Rai. 2008. 'Structures of Denial: Student Representation in Nepal's Higher Education'. *Studies in Nepali History and Society* 13(2): 235–63.

Bishop, Emily C. and Karen Willis. 2014. '"Without Hope Everything Would Be Doom and Gloom": Young People Talk about the Importance of Hope in Their Lives'. *Journal of Youth Studies* 17(6): 778–93.

Bista, Dor Bahadur. 1991. *Fatalism and Development: Nepal's Struggle for Modernization*. Hyderabad: Orient Longman.

Bourdieu, Pierre. 1977. *Outline of a Theory of Practice*. Cambridge: Cambridge University Press.

———. 1984. *Distinction: A Social Critique of the Judgement of Taste*. London: Routledge.

Brannen, Julia and Ann Nilsen. 2002. 'Young People's Time Perspectives: From Youth to Adulthood'. *Sociology* 36(3): 513–37.

Brock, Colin. 2011. *Education as a Global Concern*. London: Continuum.

Brooks, Rachel and Glyn Everett. 2008. 'The Prevalence of "Life Planning": Evidence from UK Graduates'. *British Journal of Sociology of Education* 29(3): 325–37.

Brooks, Rachel and Johanna Waters. 2011. *Student Mobilities, Migration and the Internationalization of Higher Education*. Basingstoke, NY: Palgrave Macmillan.

Brown, Gavin. 2011. 'Emotional Geographies of Young People's Aspirations for Adult Life'. *Children's Geographies* 9(1): 7–22.

Brown, Phillip, Anthony Hesketh, and Sara Williams. 2003. 'Employability in a Knowledge-driven Economy'. *Journal of Education and Work* 16(1): 107–26.

Bruslé, Tristan. 2010. 'Who's in a Labour Camp?: A Socio-economic Analysis of Nepalese Migrants in Qatar'. *European Bulletin of Himalayan Research* 35–6: 154–70.

Bucholtz, Mary. 2002. 'Youth and Cultural Practice'. *Annual Review of Anthropology* 31(1): 525–52.

Butler, Tim, Chris Hamnett, Mark Ramsden, and Richard Webber. 2007. 'The Best, the Worst and the Average: Secondary School Choice and Education Performance in East London'. *Journal of Education Policy* 22(1): 7–29.

Bynner, John, Lynne Chisholm, and Andy Furlong. 1997. *Youth, Citizenship and Social Change in a European Context*. Aldershot: Ashgate.

Caddell, Martha. 2006. 'Private Schools as Battlefields: Contested Visions of Learning and Livelihood in Nepal'. *Compare: A Journal of Comparative and International Education* 36(4): 463–79.

———. 2007. 'Education and Change: A Historical Perspective on Schooling, Development and the Nepali Nation-State'. In K. Kumar and J. Oesterheld (eds), *Education and Social Change in South Asia*, pp. 251–84. New Delhi: Orient Longman.

Cahill, Caitlin. 2007. 'Doing Research with Young People: Participatory Research and the Rituals of Collective Work'. *Children's Geographies* 5(3): 297–312.

Cameron, Mary M. 1998. *On the Edge of the Auspicious: Gender and Caste in Nepal*. Urbana: University of Illinois Press.

Caplan, Lionel. 1970. *Land and Social Change in East Nepal: A Study of Hindu-Tribal Relations*. London: Routledge & Kegan Paul.

Carney, Stephen and Ulla A. Madsen. 2009. 'A Place of One's Own: Schooling and the Formation of Identities in Modern Nepal'. In J. Zajda, H. Daun, and L.J. Saha (eds), *Nation-Building, Identity and Citizenship Education: Cross Cultural Perspectives*, pp. 171–87. Amsterdam: Kluwer Academic Publishers.

Castles, Stephen and Mark J. Miller. 2009. *The Age of Migration*. Basingstoke: Palgrave Macmillan.

Central Bureau of Statistics (CBS). 2004. *Nepal Living Standards Survey 2003/04: Statistical Report, Vol. 1*. Kathmandu: Central Bureau of Statistics.

Central Bureau of Statistics (CBS). 2011. *Nepal Living Standards Survey 2010/11: Statistical Report, Vol. 1.* Kathmandu: Central Bureau of Statistics.

———. 2013. *Nepal in Figures 2013.* Kathmandu: Central Bureau of Statistics.

Chettri, Mona. 2013. 'Choosing the Gorkha: At the Crossroads of Class and Ethnicity in the Darjeeling Hills'. *Asian Ethnicity* 14(3): 293–308.

Clark, Burton R. 1960. 'The "Cooling-Out" Function in Higher Education'. *American Journal of Sociology* 65(6): 569–76.

Clarke, John, Stuart Hall, Tony Jefferson, and Brian Roberts. 1975. 'Subcultures, Cultures and Class'. In S. Hall and T. Jefferson (eds), *Resistance through Ritual: Youth Subcultures in Post-War Britain*, pp. 9–74 London: Hutchinson.

Clifford, James. 1997. *Routes: Travel and Translation in the Late Twentieth Century.* Cambridge, MA, and London: Harvard University Press.

Cohen, Jeffrey H. and Ibrahim Sirkeci. 2011. *Cultures of Migration: The Global Nature of Contemporary Mobility.* Austin: University of Texas Press.

Cole, Jennifer. 2004. 'Fresh Contact in Tamatave, Madagascar'. *American Ethnologist* 31(4): 573–88.

———. 2010. *Sex and Salvation: Imagining the Future in Madagascar.* Chicago, IL, and London: University of Chicago Press.

Cole, Jennifer and Deborah Durham. 2008. 'Introduction: Globalization and the Temporalities of Children and Youth'. In J. Cole and D. Durham (eds), *Figuring the Future: Globalization and the Temporalities of Children and Youth*, pp. 3–23. Santa Fe, NM: School for Advanced Research Press.

Coleman, James S. 1973. *Youth: Transition to Adulthood.* Chicago, IL, and London: University of Chicago Press.

Collins, Francis Leo. 2010. 'Negotiating Un/Familiar Embodiments: Investigating the Corporeal Dimensions of South Korean International Students Mobilities in Auckland, New Zealand'. *Population, Space and Place* 16(1): 51–62.

———. 2012. 'Cyber-Spatial Mediations and Educational Mobilities: International Students and the Internet'. In R. Brooks, A. Fuller, and J. Waters (eds), *Changing Spaces of Education: New Perspectives on the Nature of Learning*, pp. 244–60. London: Routledge.

Collins, Rebecca, James Esson, Caitlin O'Neill Gutierrez, and Adefemi Adekunle. 2013. 'Youth in Motion: Spatialising Youth Movement(s) in the Social Sciences'. *Children's Geographies* 11(3): 369–76.

Cresswell, Tim. 2006. *On the Move: Mobility in the Modern Western World.* Abingdon and New York: Taylor and Francis.

———. 2010. 'Mobilities I: Catching Up'. *Progress in Human Geography* 35(4): 550–58.

Cresswell, Tim. 2010. 'Mobilities II: Still'. *Progress in Human Geography* 36(5): 645–53.

Cross, Jamie. 2010. 'From Dreams to Discontent: Educated Young Men and the Politics of Work at a Special Economic Zone in Andhra Pradesh'. *Contributions to Indian Sociology* 43(3): 351–79.

Crozier, Gill. 2009. 'South Asian Parents' Aspirations versus Teachers' Expectations in the United Kingdom'. *Theory into Practice* 48(4): 290–6.

Davidson, Elsa. 2011. *The Burdens of Aspiration: Schools, Youth, and Success in the Divided Social Worlds of Silicon Valley.* New York and London: New York University Press.

de Haan, Arjan and Ben Rogaly. 2002. 'Introduction: Migrant Workers and their Role in Rural Change'. *The Journal of Development Studies* 38(5): 1–14.

Demerath, Peter. 2003. 'Negotiating Individualist and Collectivist Futures: Emerging Subjectivities and Social Forms in Papua New Guinean High Schools'. *Anthropology & Education Quarterly* 34(2): 136–57.

Deshar, Ramesh. 2011. 'Travelling Blind'. *The Kathmandu Post*, 20 March.

Dhakal, Prem. 2009. 'Nepal's Most Expensive Schools'. *Republica*, 5 March.

Donner, Henrike. 2005. '"Children are Capital, Grandchildren are Interest": Changing Educational Strategies and Parenting in Calcutta's Middle-Class Families'. In J. Assayag and C. Fuller (eds), *Globalizing India*, pp. 119–39. London: Anthem Press.

Dore, Ronald P. 1976. *The Diploma Disease: Education, Qualification and Development.* London: Institute of Education.

du Bois-Reymond, Manuela. 1998. '"I Don't Want to Commit Myself Yet": Young People's Life Concepts'. *Journal of Youth Studies* 1(1): 63–79.

Durham, Deborah. 2008. 'Apathy and Agency: The Romance of Agency and Youth in Botswana'. In J. Cole and D. Durham (eds), *Figuring the Future: Globalization and the Temporalities of Children and Youth*, pp. 151–78. Santa Fe, NM: School for Advanced Research Press.

Dyson, Jane. 2008. 'Harvesting Identities: Youth, Work, and Gender in the Indian Himalayas'. *Annals of the Association of American Geographers* 98(1): 160–79.

———. 2010. 'Friendship in Practice: Girls' Work in the Indian Himalayas'. *American Ethnologist* 37(3): 482–98.

———. 2014. *Working Childhoods: Youth, Agency and the Working Environment in India.* Cambridge: Cambridge University Press.

Ellison, Nicole B., Charles Steinfield and Cliff Lampe. 2007. 'The Benefits of Facebook 'Friends': Social Capital and College Students' Use of Online Social Network Sites'. *Journal of Computer-Mediated Communication* 12: 1143–68

Evans, Bethan. 2008. 'Geographies of Youth/Young People'. *Geography Compass* 2(5): 1659–80.

Faye, Reidun. 2017. 'Navigating Development: An Ethnographic Study of Development Aid, Education and Social Change among Urban Squatters in Nepal'. PhD thesis, University of Bergen, Norway.

Fincher, Ruth and Kate Shaw. 2009. 'The Unintended Segregation of Transnational Students in Central Melbourne'. *Environment and Planning A* 41(8): 1884–902.

Findlay, Allan M., Russell King, Fiona M. Smith, Alistair Geddes, and Ronald Skeldon. 2012. 'World Class?: An Investigation of Globalisation, Difference and International Student Mobility'. *Transactions of the Institute of British Geographers* 37(1): 118–31.

Fischer, Peter and Gunnar Malmberg. 2001. 'Settled People Don't Move: On Life Course and (Im-)Mobility in Sweden'. *International Journal of Population Geography* 7(5): 357–71.

Flanagan, Constance A. and Nakesha Faison. 2001. 'Youth Civic Development: Implications for Social Policy and Programs'. *Social Policy Report* 15(1): 3–14.

Fortier, Anne-Marie. 2014. 'Migration Studies'. In P. Adey, D. Bissell, K. Hannam, P. Merriman, and M. Sheller (eds), *Routledge Handbook of Mobilities*, pp. 64–73. London: Taylor and Francis.

France, Alan. 2007. *Understanding Youth in Late Modernity*. Maidenhead: Open University Press.

Frederiksen, Bodil F. 2002. 'Mobile Minds and Socio-economic Barriers: Livelihoods and African-American Identifications among Youth in Nairobi'. In N.N. Sørensen and K.F. Olwig (eds), *Work and Migration: Life and Livelihoods in a Globalizing World*, pp. 45–60. London: Routledge.

Froerer, Peggy and Anna Portisch. 2012. 'Introduction to the Special Issue: Learning, Livelihoods, and Social Mobility'. *Anthropology & Education Quarterly* 43(4): 332–43.

Furlong, Andy and Fred Cartmel. 1997. *Young People and Social Change: Individualization and Risk in Late Modernity*. Buckingham and Philadelphia, PA: Open University Press.

Geisen, Thomas. 2010. 'New Perspectives on Youth and Migration: Belonging, Cultural Repositioning and Social Mobility'. In D. Crains (ed.), *Youth on the Move: European Youth and Geographical Mobility*, pp. 11–21. Wiesbaden: VS Verlag für Sozialwissenschaften.

Gellner, David. 2004. 'Children's Voices from Kathmandu and Lalitpur, Nepal'. *Journal of Asian and African Studies* 68: 1–46.

Ghale, Ngawang T. 2011. 'We Make the Nation'. *Wave*, June.

Ghimire, Anita. 2010. 'Caught between Two Worlds: Internal Displacement Induced Dilemma in Nepal'. *European Bulletin of Himalayan Research* 35–6: 91–106.

Ghimire, Anita and Kabin Maharjan. 2015. 'Student Returnees and Their Reflection on Contribution to Nepal: Use of Knowledge and Skills'. *Migration and Development* 4(1): 90–107.

Ghimire, Binod. 2015. 'Foreign Degree Seekers Hit Record Number'. *The Kathmandu Post*, 28 July.

Ghimire, Krishna B. 2005. 'Social Movements and Marginalized Rural Youth in Brazil, Egypt andNepal'. *The Journal of Peasant Studies* 30(1): 30–72.

Goffman, Erving. 1952. 'On Cooling the Mark Out: Some Aspects of Adaptation to Failure'. *Psychiatry* 15(4): 451–63.

Goldin, Ian, Geoffrey Cameron, and Meera Balarajan. 2011. *Exceptional People: How Migration Shaped Our World and Will Define Our Future.* Princeton, NJ, and Oxford: Princeton University Press.

Graner, Elvira. 2001. 'Labor Markets and Migration in Nepal: The Case of Workers in Kathmandu Valley Carpet Manufactories'. *Mountain Research and Development* 21(3): 253–9.

———. 2010. 'Leaving Hills and Plains: Migration and Remittances in Nepal'. *European Bulletin of Himalayan Research* 35–6: 24–42.

Graner, Elvira and Ganesh Gurung. 2003. 'Arab ko Lahure: Nepalese Labour Migration to Arabian Countries'. *Contributions to Nepalese Studies* 30(2): 295–325.

Gurung, Ganesh. 2003. 'Foreign Employment and Remittance Economy of Nepal'. In M. Domrös (ed.), *Translating Development: The Case of Nepal,* pp. 266–81. New Delhi: Social Science Press.

Hall, G. Stanley. 1904. *Adolescence: Its Psychology and Its Relations to Physiology, Anthropology, Sociology, Sex, Crime, Religion and Education.* New York: D. Appleton and Company.

Hall, Stuart and Tony Jefferson, eds. 1975 *Resistance through Rituals: Youth Subcultures in Post-War Britain.* London: Hutchinson.

Hammer, Tomas and Kristof Tamas. 1997. 'Why Do People Go or Stay?' In T. Hammer (ed.), *International Migration, Immobility and Development: Multidisciplinary Perspectives,* pp. 1–19. Oxford: Berg.

Hamnett, Chris and Tim Butler. 2011. '"Geography Matters": The Role Distance Plays in Reproducing Educational Inequality in East London'. *Transactions of the Institute of British Geographers* 36(4): 479–500.

Hannam, Kevin, Mimi Sheller, and John Urry. 2006. 'Editorial: Mobilities, Immobilities and Moorings'. *Mobilities* 1(1): 1–22.

Hannerz, Ulf. 1996. *Transnational Connections: Culture, People, Places.* London: Routledge.

Hansen, Karen Tranberg. 2005. 'Getting Stuck in the Compound: Some Odds against Social Adulthood in Lusaka, Zambia'. *Africa Today* 51(4): 3–16.

Hanson Thiem, Claudia. 2009. 'Thinking through Education: The Geographies of Contemporary Educational Restructuring'. *Progress in Human Geography* 33(2): 154–73.

Harris, Richard. 2013. 'Geographies of Transition and the Separation of Lower and Higher Attaining Pupils in the Move from Primary to Secondary School in London'. *Transactions of the Institute of British Geographers* 38(2): 254–66.

Hayden, Mary. 2011. 'Transnational Spaces of Education: The Growth of the International School Sector'. *Globalisation, Societies and Education* 9(2): 211–24.

Heaton Shrestha, Celayne. 2002. 'NGOs as Thekadars or Sevaks?: Identity Crisis in Nepal's Non-governmental Sector'. *European Bulletin of Himalayan Research* 22: 5–36.

———. 2010. 'Let's Do a Rethink'. *The Kathmandu Post*, 4 January.

Heaton Shrestha, Celayne and Ramesh Adhikari. 2011. 'NGOization and De-NGOization of Public Action in Nepal: The Role of Organizational Culture in Civil Society Politicality'. *Journal of Civil Society* 7(1): 41–61.

Heinz, Walter R. 1987. 'The Transition from School to Work in Crisis: Coping with Threatening Unemployment'. *Journal of Adolescent Research* 2(2): 127–41.

———. 2003. 'From Work Trajectories to Negotiated Careers: The Contingent Life Course'. In J.T. Mortimer and M.J. Shanahan (eds), *Handbook of the Life Course*, pp. 185–204. New York: Kluwer Academic Publishers.

Hindman, Heather and Bijaya Raj Poudel. 2015. 'Can Nepal's Youth Build Back Better and Differently?' *Cultural Anthropology*, 14 October. Available at http://www.culanth.org/fieldsights/733-can-nepal-s-youth-build-back-better-and-differently, accessed 10 February 2016.

Hirslund, Dan V. 2012. 'Sacrificing Youth: Maoist Cadres and Political Activism in Post-War Nepal'. PhD thesis, University of Copenhagen, Denmark.

Hoechner, Hannah. 2011. 'Striving for Knowledge and Dignity: How Qur'anic Students in Kano, Nigeria, Learn to Live with Rejection and Educational Disadvantage'. *European Journal of Development Research* 23(5): 712–28.

Hoffman, Thomas. 2001. 'Out-migration Patterns of Solu-Khumbu District'. In S. von der Heide and T. Hoffman (eds), *Aspects of Migration and Mobility in Nepal*, pp. 115–28. Kathmandu: Ratna Pustak Bhandar.

Hoftun, Martin, William Raeper, and John Whelpton. 1999. *People, Politics & Ideology: Democracy and Social Change in Nepal*. Kathmandu: Mandala Book Point.

Højlund, Susanne, Lotte Meinert, Martin Demant Frederiksen, and Anne Line Dalsgaard. 2011. 'Well-Faring towards Uncertain Futures: A Comparative Perspective on Youth in Marginalized Positions'. *Anthropology in Action* 18(3): 45–56.

Holdsworth, Clare. 2009. '"Going Away to Uni": Mobility, Modernity, and Independence of English Higher Education Students'. *Environment and Planning A* 41(8): 1849–64.

Holloway, Sarah L., Phil Hubbard, Heike Jons, and Helena Pimlott-Wilson. 2010. 'Geographies of Education and the Significance of Children, Youth and Families'. *Progress in Human Geography* 34(5): 583–600.

Holloway, Sarah L. and Heike Jöns. 2012. 'Geographies of Education and Learning'. *Transactions of the Institute of British Geographers* 37(4): 482–8.

Holloway, Sarah L. and Helena Pimlott-Wilson. 2011. 'The Politics of Aspiration: Neo-Liberal Education Policy, "Low" Parental Aspirations, and Primary School Extended Services in Disadvantaged Communities'. *Children's Geographies* 9(1): 79–94.

Holloway, Sarah L. and Gill Valentine. 2000a. 'Corked Hats and Coronation Street: British and New Zealand Children's Imaginative Geographies of the Other'. *Childhood* 7(3): 335–57.

———. 2000b. 'Spatiality and the New Social Studies of Childhood'. *Sociology* 34(4): 763–83.

Honwana, Alcinda M. and Filip de Boeck, eds. 2005. *Makers and Breakers: Children and Youth in Postcolonial Africa*. Oxford: James Currey.

Hopkins, Peter and Rachel Pain. 2007. 'Geographies of Age: Thinking Relationally'. *Area* 39(3): 287–94.

Hörschelmann, Kathrin. 2011. 'Theorising Life Transitions: Geographical Perspectives'. *Area* 43(4): 378–83.

Horton, John and Peter Kraftl. 2005. 'For More-than-Usefulness: Six Overlapping Points about Children's Geographies'. *Children's Geographies* 3(2): 131–43.

———. 2006. 'What Else?: Some More Ways of Thinking and Doing "Children's Geographies"'. *Children's Geographies* 4(1): 69–95.

Institute of International Education (IIE). 2011. *Open Doors Report on International Educational Exchange 2010/2011*. New York: Institute of International Education. Available at http://www.iie.org/opendoors, accessed 29 December 2019.

Jad, Islah. 2007. 'NGOs: Between Buzzwords and Social Movements'. *Development in Practice* 17(4–5): 622–9.

James, Allison, Chris Jenks, and Alan Prout. 1998. *Theorizing Childhood*. Cambridge: Polity Press.

Jeffrey, Craig. 2010a. 'Geographies of Children and Youth I: Eroding Maps of Life'. *Progress in Human Geography* 34(4): 496–505.

———. 2010b. *Timepass: Youth, Class, and the Politics of Waiting in India.* Stanford: Stanford University Press.

Jeffrey, Craig, Patricia Jeffery, and Roger Jeffery. 2008. *Degrees without Freedom?: Education, Masculinities and Unemployment in North India.* Stanford: Stanford University Press.

Jenkins, Richard. 1983. *Lads, Citizens and Ordinary Kids: Working-Class Youth Life-Styles in Belfast.* London: Routledge & Kegan Paul.

Johnson-Hanks, Jennifer. 2002. 'On the Limits of Life Stages in Ethnography: Toward a Theory of Vital Conjunctures'. *American Anthropologist* 104(3): 865–80.

———. 2005. 'When the Future Decides: Uncertainty and Intentional Action in Contemporary Cameroon'. *Current Anthropology* 46(3): 363–85.

Kayastha, Narendra. 1985. *University Education and Employment in Nepal.* Kathmandu: Centre for Economic Development and Administration, Tribhuvan University.

Khare, Shagun and Anja Slany. 2011. *The Dynamics of Employment, the Labour Market and the Economy in Nepal.* Geneva: International Labour Office.

Kölbel, Andrea. 2013. '(De)Valuing Higher Education: Educated Youth, Generational Differences and a Changing Educational Landscape in Kathmandu, Nepal'. *Comparative Education* 49(3): 331–43.

———. 2015. 'Youth, Aspiration, and Mobility: Young People Debating their Potential Futures in Nepal'. PhD thesis, University of Oxford, UK.

———. 2016. 'Nepal's Educated Non-Elite: Re-evaluating State-provided Higher Education'. In M. Shah and G. Whiteford (eds), *Bridges, Pathways and Transitions: International Innovations in Widening Participation*, pp. 173–88. Oxford: Chandos Publishing/Elsevier.

———. 2017. 'A History of Higher Education in Nepal: From Urban Elitism to Global Aspirations'. In H. Letchamanan and D. Dhar (eds), *Education in South Asia and the Indian Ocean Islands*, pp. 183–201. London: Bloomsbury.

———. 2018. 'Imaginative Geographies of International Student Mobility'. *Social & Cultural Geography.* Available at https://www.tandfonline.com/doi/full/10.1080/14649365.2018.1460861, accessed 29 December 2019.

Kraftl, Peter. 2008. 'Young People, Hope, and Childhood-Hope'. *Space and Culture* 11(2): 81–92.

Kunreuther, Laura. 2006. 'Technologies of the Voice: FM Radio, Telephone, and the Nepali Diaspora in Kathmandu'. *Cultural Anthropology* 21(3): 323–53.

Lal, C.K. 2000. 'Continuing Confusion in Nepal'. Indian Seminar Series. Available at http://www.india-seminar.com/2000/494/494c.k.lal.htm, accessed 27 May 2015.

Lave, Jean, Paul Duguid, Nadine Fernandez, and Erik Axel. 1992. 'Coming of Age in Birmingham: Cultural Studies and Conceptions of Subjectivity'. *Annual Review of Anthropology* 21(1): 257–82.

Lee, Jenny J. 2008. 'Beyond Borders: International Student Pathways to the United States'. *Journal of Studies in International Education* 12(3): 308–27.

Liechty, Mark. 2003. *Suitably Modern: Making Middle-Class Culture in a New Consumer Society*. Princeton, NJ, and Oxford: Princeton University Press.

———. 2010. *Out Here in Kathmandu: Modernity on the Global Periphery*. Kathmandu: Martin Chautari Press.

Lind Petersen, Birgitte. 2011. 'Becoming Citizens: Youth, Schooling and Citizenship in Post-War Rural Nepal'. PhD thesis, University of Copenhagen, Denmark.

Little, Angela W. and Keith M. Lewin. 2011. 'The Policies, Politics and Progress of Access to Basic Education'. *Journal of Education Policy* 26(4): 477–82.

Lloyd, Cynthia B. 2005. *Growing Up Global: The Changing Transitions to Adulthood in Developing Countries*. Washington, DC: The National Academies Press.

Lowe, John. 2000. 'International Examinations: The New Credentialism and Reproduction of Advantage in a Globalising World'. *Assessment in Education: Principles, Policy & Practice* 7(3): 363–77.

Lukose, Ritty. 2010. *Liberalization's Children: Gender, Youth, and Consumer Citizenship in Globalizing India*. Durham, NC: Duke University Press.

Madge, Clare, Parvati Raghuram, and Patricia Noxolo. 2009. 'Engaged Pedagogy and Responsibility: A Postcolonial Analysis of International Students'. *Geoforum* 40(1): 34–45.

———. 2015. 'Conceptualizing International Education: From International Student to International Study'. *Progress in Human Geography* 39(6): 681–701.

Madsen, Ulla A. and Stephen Carney. 2011. 'Education in an Age of Radical Uncertainty: Youth and Schooling in Urban Nepal'. *Globalisation, Societies and Education* 9(1): 115–33.

Magazine, Roger and Martha Areli Ramírez Sánchez. 2007. 'Continuity and Change in San Pedro Tlalcuapan, Mexico: Childhood, Social Reproduction, and Transnational Migration'. In J. Cole and D.L. Durham (eds), *Generations and Globalization: Youth, Age, and Family in the New World Economy*, pp. 52–73. Bloomington: Indiana University Press.

Mahmood, Saba. 2005. *Politics of Piety: The Islamic Revival and the Feminist Subject*. Princeton, NJ, and Oxford: Princeton University Press.

Mains, Daniel. 2012. *Hope Is Cut: Youth, Unemployment, and the Future in Urban Ethiopia*. Philadelphia, PA: Temple University Press.

Majupuria, Trilok Chandra and Indra Majupuria. 1985. *Youth of Nepal*. Gwalior: M. Devi.

Mandelbaum, David G. 1973. 'The Study of Life History: Gandhi'. *Current Anthropology* 14(3): 177–93.

Mannheim, Karl. [1923] 1952. 'The Problem of Generations'. In P. Kecskemeti (ed.), *Essays on the Sociology of Knowledge*, Vol. 57, pp. 276–320. London: Routledge & Kegan Paul.

Marginson, Simon and Marijk van der Wende. 2007. 'To Rank or to Be Ranked: The Impact of Global Rankings in Higher Education'. *Journal of Studies in International Education* 11(3–4): 306–29.

Masquelier, Adeline. 2005. 'The Scorpion's Sting: Youth, Marriage and the Struggle for Social Maturity in Niger'. *Journal of the Royal Anthropological Institute* 11(1): 59–83.

Massey, Doreen. 1993. 'Power-Geometry and a Progressive Sense of Place'. In J. Bird, B. Curtis, T. Putnam, G. Robertson, and L. Tickner (eds), *Mapping the Futures: Local Cultures, Global Change*, pp. 59–69. London and New York: Routledge.

Matthews, Hugh, Melanie Limb, and Mark Taylor. 1999. 'Young People's Participation and Representation in Society'. *Geoforum* 30(2): 135–44.

McDowell, Linda. 2003. *Redundant Masculinities?: Employment Change and White Working Class Youth*. Oxford: Blackwell.

Meinert, Lotte. 2009. *Hopes in Friction: Schooling, Health and Everyday Life in Uganda*. Charlotte, NC: Information Age Publishing.

Messerschmidt, Don, Gautam Yadama, and Bhuvan Silwal. 2007. 'History and Significance of National Development Service (NDS): Creating "Civic Space" and Commitment to Service in Nepal during the 1970s'. *Occasional Papers in Sociology and Anthropology* 10: 174–207.

Michaels, Axel. 2004. *Hinduism: Past and Present*. Princeton, NJ, and Oxford: Princeton University Press.

Mikesell, Stephen. 2006. 'Thoughts on Why the Children of Nepal Would Join the Revolution'. In R. K. Vishwakarma (ed.), *People's Power in Nepal*, pp. 53–8. New Delhi: Manak Publishing.

Ministry of Education (MoE). 1970. *Development of Higher Education in Nepal*. Kathmandu: Ministry of Education.

Ministry of Youth and Sports (MoYS). 2010. *National Youth Policy*. Kathmandu: Ministry of Youth and Sports.

Morley, David. 2000. *Home Territories: Media, Mobility and Identity*. London: Routledge.

Muzzini, Elisa and Gabriela Aparicio. 2013. *Urban Growth and Spatial Transition in Nepal: An Initial Assessment*. Washington, DC: The World Bank.

Nelson, Andrew. 2013. *The Mobility of Permanence: The Progress of Relocating to Kathmandu*. Kathmandu: Centre for the Study of Labour and Mobility. Available at https://soscbaha.org/ebook/the-mobility-of-permanence-the-process-of-relocating-to-kathmandu/, accessed 29 December 2019.

Newell, Sasha. 2012. *The Modernity Bluff: Crime, Consumption, and Citizenship in Côte d'Ivoire*. Chicago, IL, and London: University of Chicago Press.

Nisbett, Nicholas. 2007. 'Friendship, Consumption, Morality: Practising Identity, Negotiating Hierarchy in Middle-Class Bangalore'. *Journal of the Royal Anthropological Institute* 13(4): 935–50.

Olwig, Karen Fog and Karen Valentin. 2015. 'Mobility, Education and Life Trajectories: New and Old Migratory Pathways'. *Identities* 22(3): 247–57.

Ortner, Sherry B. 2006. *Anthropology and Social Theory*. Durham, NC, and London: Duke University Press.

Osella, Filippo and Caroline Osella. 2000. 'Migration, Money and Masculinity in Kerala'. *Journal of the Royal Anthropological Institute* 6(1): 117–33.

Pain, Rachel, Ruth Panelli, Sara Kindon, and Jo Little. 2010. 'Moments in Everyday/Distant Geopolitics: Young People's Fears and Hopes'. *Geoforum* 41(6): 972–82.

Panday, Devendra Raj. 1999. *Nepal's Failed Development: Reflections on the Mission and the Maladies*. Kathmandu: Nepal South Asia Centre.

Parry, Jonathan. P. 2003. 'Nehru's Dream and the Village "Waiting Room": Long-Distance Labour Migrants to a Central Indian Steel Town'. *Contributions to Indian Sociology* 37(1–2): 217–49.

Pettigrew, Judith. 2007. 'Learning to Be Silent'. In Hiroshi Ishii, David Gellner, and, Katsuo Nawa (eds), *Social Dynamics in Northern South Asia: Nepalis inside and outside Nepal*, pp. 307–48. New Delhi: Manohar Publishers.

Pherali, Tejendra J. 2011. 'Education and Conflict in Nepal: Possibilities for Reconstruction'. *Globalisation, Societies and Education* 9(1): 135–54.

Pigg, Stacy Leigh. 1992. 'Investing Social Categories through Place: Social Representations and Development in Nepal'. *Comparative Studies in Society and History* 34(3): 491–513.

Poudel, Bhoj Raj and Pieter de Schepper. 2010. *Generation Dialogues— Youth in Politics: Nepal.* Kathmandu: Youth Initiative.

Poudel, Suman Babu and Anita Ghimire. 2010. 'Internally Displaced Persons'. In *Nepal Migration Year Book 2009*, pp. 60–70. Kathmandu: Nepal Institute of Development Studies and National Centre of Competence in Research.

Punch, Samantha. 2002. 'Youth Transitions and Interdependent Adult–Child Relations in Rural Bolivia'. *Journal of Rural Studies* 18(2): 123–33.

Raco, Mike. 2009. 'From Expectations to Aspirations: State Modernisation, Urban Policy, and the Existential Politics of Welfare in the UK'. *Political Geography* 28(7): 436–44.

Ralph, Michael. 2008. 'Killing Time'. *Social Text* 26(4): 1–29.

Rankin, Katharine N. 2003. 'Cultures of Economies: Gender and Socio-spatial Change in Nepal'. *Gender, Place & Culture* 10(2): 111–29.

———. 2004. *The Cultural Politics of Markets: Economic Liberalization and Social Change in Nepal.* London: Pluto Press.

Rao, Nitya. 2010. 'Aspiring for Distinction: Gendered Educational Choices in an Indian Village'. *Compare: A Journal of Comparative and International Education* 40(2): 167–83.

Rao, Nitya and Munshi Israil Hossain. 2012. '"I Want to be Respected": Migration, Mobility, and the Construction of Alternate Educational Discourses in Rural Bangladesh'. *Anthropology & Education Quarterly* 43(4): 415–28.

Reay, Diane. 2008. 'Tony Blair, the Promotion of the "Active" Educational Citizen, and Middle-Class Hegemony'. *Oxford Review of Education* 34(February): 639–50.

Regmi, Mahesh Chandra. 1978. *Land Tenure and Taxation in Nepal.* Kathmandu: Ratna Pustak Bhandar.

Republica. 2012. 'UN Urges for Policies to Turn Brain Drain into Brain Gain', 29 November.

Reynolds, Pamela. 1991. *Dance Civet Cat: Child Labour in the Zambezi Valley.* London: Zed Books Ltd.

Rizvi, Fazal. 2000. 'International Education and the Production of a Global Imagination'. In N. Burbules and C.A. Torres (eds), *Globalisation and Education: Critical Perspectives*, pp. 205–25. New York: Routledge.

———. 2011. 'Theorizing Student Mobility in an Era of Globalization'. *Teachers and Teaching: Theory and Practice* 17(6): 693–701.

Roberts, Ken. 2007. 'Youth Transitions and Generations: A Response to Wyn and Woodman'. *Journal of Youth Studies* 10(2): 263–9.

Roberts, Ken, Stephen C. Clark, and Claire Wallace. 1994. 'Flexibility and Individualisation: A Comparison of Transitions into Employment in England and Germany'. *Sociology* 28(1): 31–54.

Rockwell, Elsie. 1996. 'Keys to Appropriation: Rural Schooling in Mexico'. In B.A. Levinson, D.A. Foley, and D. Holland (eds), *The Cultural Production of the Educated Person: Critical Ethnographies of Schooling and Local Practice*, pp. 301–24. Albany, NY: State University of New York Press.

Ruddick, Sue. 2003. 'The Politics of Aging: Globalization and the Restructuring of Youth and Childhood'. *Antipode* 35(2): 334–62.

Salazar, Noel B. 2011. 'The Power of Imagination in Transnational Mobilities'. *Identities* 18(6): 576–98.

Scott, James C. 1986. 'Everyday Forms of Peasant Resistance'. *Journal of Peasant Studies* 13(2): 5–35.

Seddon, David, Jagannath Adhikari, and Ganesh Gurung. 2001. *The New Lahures: Foreign Employment and Remittance Economy of Nepal*. Kathmandu: Nepal Institute of Development Studies.

———. 2002. 'Foreign Labor Migration and the Remittance Economy of Nepal'. *Critical Asian Studies* 34(1): 19–40.

Shakya, Keshab Man. 2008. 'Foreign Aid, Democracy, and Development'. In D. Gellner and K. Hachhethu (eds), *Local Democracy in South Asia: Microprocesses of Democratization in Nepal and its Neighbours*, pp. 258–75. London and New Delhi: Sage.

Shanahan, Michael J. 2000. 'Pathways to Adulthood in Changing Societies: Variability and Mechanisms in Life Course Perspective'. *Annual Review of Sociology* 26(1): 667–92.

Sharma, Jeevan Raj. 2009. 'Practices of Male Labor Migration from the Hills of Nepal to India in Development Discourses: Which Pathology?' *Gender, Technology and Development* 12(3): 303–23.

———. 2010. 'Understanding the Nepali Exodus'. *Republica*, 31 December.

———. 2012. 'Nepal: Migration History and Trends'. In I. Sirkeci, J.H. Cohen, and D. Ratha (eds), *Migration and Remittances during the Global Financial Crisis and Beyond*, pp. 137–40. Washington, DC: The World Bank.

Sheller, Mimi and John Urry. 2006. 'The New Mobilities Paradigm'. *Environment and Planning A* 38(2): 207–26.

Sherpa, Phudorji. 2002. 'A Nation's Call'. *Nepali Times*, November.

Shrestha, Min Bahadur and Shashi Kant Chaudhary. 2013. *The Economic Cost of General Strikes in Nepal*. Kathmandu: Nepal Rastra Bank.

Shrestha, Nanda R. 1990. *Landlessness and Migration in Nepal*. Boulder, CO, and Oxford: Westview Press.

Shrestha, Ratna Sansar. 2010. 'Electricity Crisis (Load Shedding) in Nepal, Its Manifestations and Ramifications'. *Hydro Nepal* 6: 7–17.

Sijapati, Bandita. 2005. 'Perils of Higher Education Reform in Nepal'. *Journal of Development and Social Transformation* 2: 25–33.

Sijapati, Bandita and Margaret G. Hermann. 2012. 'Learning Democracy: International Education and Political Socialization.' In S.S. Brown (ed.),

Transnational Transfers and Global Development, pp. 148–62. Basingstoke and New York: Palgrave Macmillan.

Sijapati Basnett, Bimbika. 2012. 'The Development Industry'. *Nepali Times*, September.

Skelton, Tracey and Gill Valentine. 1997. *Cool Places: Geographies of Youth Cultures*. London: Routledge.

Skinner, Debra. 1990. 'Nepalese Children's Construction of Identities in and around Formal Schooling'. *Himalayan Research Bulletin* 10(2–3): 8–17.

Skinner, Debra and Dorothy Holland. 1996. 'Schools and the Cultural Production of the Educated Person in a Nepalese Hill Community'. In B.A. Levinson, D.E. Foley, and D.C. Holland (eds), *The Cultural Production of the Educated Person: Critical Ethnographies of Schooling and Local Practice*, pp. 273–300. Albany, NY: State University of New York Press.

Smith, Darren P., Patrick Rérat, and Joanna Sage. 2014. 'Youth Migration and Spaces of Education'. *Children's Geographies* 12(1): 1–8.

Smith, Sara H. 2013. '"In the Heart, There's Nothing": Unruly Youth, Generational Vertigo and Territory'. *Transactions of the Institute of British Geographers* 38(4): 572–85.

Snellinger, Amanda. 2005. 'A Crisis in Nepali Student Politics?: Analyzing the Gap between Politically Active and Non-active Students'. *Peace and Democracy in South Asia* 1(2): 14–30.

———. 2007. 'Student Movements in Nepal: Their Parameters and their Idealized Forms'. In M. Lawoti (ed.), *Contentious Politics and Democratization in Nepal*, pp. 273–95. Los Angeles, CA, and London: SAGE.

———. 2009. 'Yuba, Hamro Pusta: Youth and Generational Politics in Nepali Political Culture'. *Studies in Nepali History and Society* 14(1): 39–66.

———. 2010. 'Transfiguration of the Political: Nepali Student Activism and the Politics of Acculturation'. PhD thesis, Cornell University, New York.

———. 2013. 'Shaping a Livable Present and Future: A Review of Youth Studies in Nepal'. *European Bulletin of Himalayan Research* 42: 75–103.

———. 2018. *Making New Nepal: From Student Activism to Mainstream Politics*. Seattle: University of Washington Press.

Sommers, Marc. 2012. *Stuck: Rwandan Youth and the Struggle for Adulthood*. Athens: University of Georgia Press.

Sørensen, Ninna Nyberg and Karen Fog Olwig. 2002. *Work and Migration: Life and Livelihoods in a Globalizing World*. London: Routledge.

Stambach, Amy. 2000. *Lessons from Mount Kilimanjaro: Schooling, Community and Gender in East Africa*. New York and London: Routledge.

Subedi, Bhim Prasad. 1999. 'An Anthropo-geographic Approach to Territorial Mobility: Examples from Inside a Rural Nepali Community'. In R.B. Chhetri and O.P. Gurung (eds), *Anthropology and Sociology of Nepal: Cultures, Societies, Ecology and Development*, pp. 122–50. Kathmandu: Sociological and Anthropological Society of Nepal.

Swanson, Kate. 2010. *Begging as a Path to Progress: Indigenous Women and Children and the Struggle for Ecuador's Urban Spaces*. Atlanta, GA: University of Georgia Press.

Thapa, Amrit. 2015. 'Public and Private School Performance in Nepal: An Analysis Using the SLC Examination'. *Education Economics* 23(1): 47–62.

———. 2013. 'Does Private School Competition Improve Public School Performance?: The Case of Nepal'. *International Journal of Educational Development* 33(4): 358–66.

The Kathmandu Post. 2011. 'Per Capita Income Up', 7 July.

Thieme, Susan and Simone Wyss. 2005. 'Migration Patterns and Remittance Transfer in Nepal: A Case Study of Sainik Basti in Western Nepal'. *International Migration* 43(5): 59–98.

Thomson, Rachel, Robert Bell, Janet Holland, Sheila Henderson, Sheena McGrellis, and Sue Sharpe. 2002. 'Critical Moments: Choice, Chance and Opportunity in Young People's Narratives of Transition'. *Sociology* 36(2): 335–54.

Tribhuvan University (TU). 1996. *Tribhuvan University: A Historical Profile*. Kathmandu: Tribhuvan University.

———. 2012. 'About Us'. Kathmandu: Tribhuvan University. Available at http://www.tribhuvanuniversity.edu.np/index.php?option=com_content&view=article&id=173&Itemid=232, accessed 25 July 2012.

Turner, Victor. 1969. *The Ritual Process: Structure and Anti-Structure*. Chicago, IL: Aldine.

———. 1974. 'Liminal to Liminoid, in Play, Flow and Ritual: An Essay in Comparative Symbology'. *Rice University Studies* 60(3): 53–92.

Valentin, Karen. 2005. *Schooled for the Future?: Educational Policy and Everyday Life among Urban Squatters in Nepal*. Greenwich, CT: Information Age Publishing.

———. 2011. 'Modernity, Education and Its Alternatives: Schooling among the Urban Poor in Kathmandu'. *Globalisation, Societies and Education* 9(1): 99–113.

———. 2012a. 'Caught between Internationalisation and Immigration: The Case of Nepalese Students in Denmark'. *Learning and Teaching* 5(3): 56–74.

Valentin, Karen. 2012b. 'The Role of Education in Mobile Livelihoods: Social and Geographical Routes of Young Nepalese Migrants in India'. *Anthropology & Education Quarterly* 43(4): 429–42.

———. 2015. 'Transnational education and the remaking of social identity: Nepalese student migration to Denmark.' *Identities: Global Studies in Culture and Power* 22(3): 318–32.

Valentine, Gill. 2003. 'Boundary Crossings: Transitions from Childhood to Adulthood'. *Children's Geographies* 1(1): 37–52.

van Gennep, Arnold. [1903] 1960. *The Rites of Passage*. London: Routledge & Kegan Paul.

Vanderbeck, Robert M. 2007. 'Intergenerational Geographies: Age Relations, Segregation and Re-engagements'. *Geography Compass* 1(2): 200–21.

Vanderbeck, Robert M. and Cheryl Morse Dunkley. 2003. 'Young People's Narratives of Rural–Urban Difference'. *Children's Geographies* 1(2): 241–59.

Verkaaik, Oskar. 2004. *Migrants and Militants: Fun and Urban Violence in Pakistan*. Princeton, NJ: Princeton University Press.

Vigh, Henrik. 2006. *Navigating Terrains of War: Youth and Soldiering in Guinea-Bissau*. New York and Oxford: Berghahn.

Waters, Johanna. 2006. 'Emergent Geographies of International Education and Social Exclusion'. *Antipode* 38(5): 1046–68.

———. 2009. 'In Pursuit of Scarcity: Transnational Students, "Employability", and the MBA'. *Environment and Planning A* 41(8): 1865–83.

———. 2012. 'Geographies of International Education: Mobilities and the Reproduction of Social (Dis)Advantage.' *Geography Compass* 6(3): 123–36.

Waters, Johanna and Maggi Leung. 2013. 'Immobile Transnationalisms?: Young People and Their in situ Experiences of "International" Education in Hong Kong'. *Urban Studies* 50(3): 606–20.

———. 2014. '"These Are Not the Best Students": Continuing Education, Transnationalisation and Hong Kong's Young Adult "Educational Non-Elite"'. *Children's Geographies* 12(1): 56–69.

Weiss, Brad. 2004. 'Contentious Future: Past and Present'. In B. Weiss (ed.), *Producing African Futures: Ritual and Reproduction in a Neoliberal Age*, pp. 1–20. Leiden: Brill.

Whelpton, John. 2005. *A History of Nepal*. Cambridge: Cambridge University Press.

Willis, Paul E. 1977. *Learning to Labour: How Working Class Kids Get Working Class Jobs*. Farnborough: Saxon House.

Woodman, Dan. 2013. 'Researching "Ordinary" Young People in a Changing World: The Sociology of Generations and the "Missing Middle" in Youth Research'. *Sociological Research Online* 18(1). Available at https://doi.org/10.5153%2Fsro.2868, accessed 29 December 2019.

World Bank. 2007. *World Development Report: The Next Generation*. Washington, DC: The World Bank.

————. 2018. 'Youth Summit 2018: Unleashing the Power of Human Capital'. Available at https://www.worldbank.org/en/events/2018/07/25/world-bank-youth-summit-2018-unleashing-the-power-of-human-capital, accessed 27 January 2019.

Wulff, Helena. 1995. 'Introducing Youth Culture in its Own Right: The State of the Art and New Possibilities'. In V. Amit and H. Wulff (eds), *Youth Cultures: A Cross-Cultural Perspective*, pp. 1–18. London: Routledge.

Wyn, Johanna and Dan Woodman. 2006. 'Generation, Youth and Social Change in Australia'. *Journal of Youth Studies* 9(5): 495–514.

————. 2007. 'Researching Youth in a Context of Social Change: A Reply to Roberts'. *Journal of Youth Studies* 10(3): 373–81.

Xiang, Biao and Wei Shen. 2009. 'International Student Migration and Social Stratification in China'. *International Journal of Educational Development* 29(5): 513–22.

Yoon, Kyongwon. 2006. 'Cultural Practices of "Ordinary" Youth: Transitions to Adulthood in South Korea'. *Asian Studies Review* 30(4): 375–88.

Zharkevich, Ina. 2009. 'Becoming a Maoist in a Time of Insurgency: Youth in Nepal's "People's War"'. PhD thesis, University of Oxford, UK.

Index

About the Author

Andrea Kölbel is a research fellow at the Institute for Innovation and Technology, Berlin, Germany. She holds a doctorate in human geography from the University of Oxford, UK, and a master's degree in business management from the Central European University in Budapest, Hungary. As a social and economic scientist, she is specifically interested in the changing nature of higher education, spatial (im)mobilities, social theory, and participative research methods. With her research into young people's lives and social inequalities, she builds upon her professional experiences in planning, implementation, and evaluation of education programmes on behalf of universities, ministries of education and research, and the UN Refugee Agency in countries in Asia, Africa, Europe, and the Middle East.